RESEARCH HIGHLIGHTS IN SOCIAL WORK 8

Evaluation 2nd Edition

Jessica Kingsley Publishers

Editor: Joyce Lishman
Secretary: Margaret Donald
Editorial Adviser: Professor G. Rochford
University of Aberdeen
Department of Social Work
King's College
Aberdeen

First published in 1984 by Department of Social Work
University of Aberdeen
Second edition published in 1988 by Jessica Kingsley Publishers Ltd,
13 Brunswick Centre, London WC1

British Library Cataloguing in Publication Data

Evaluation.—2nd ed.—(Research highlights
in social work; 8).
1. Social service—Research 2. Evaluation
research (Social action programs)
I. Lishman, Joyce II. Series
361'.0072 HV11

ISBN 1-85302-006-0

Printed and bound in Great Britain by
Biddles Ltd, Guildford and King's Lynn

LIST OF CONTENTS

Contributors

Joyce Lishman	Her Ph.D. research at Aberdeen University analyses social workers' behaviour in interviews using video tapes and explores the relationship between this behaviour and prognosis and outcome. Previously a social worker in child and adolescent psychiatry. Publications include 'A Clash in Perspective? A Study of Worker and Client Perceptions of Social Work' British Journal of Social Work. 8, 3, 1974, a study of her own practice.
Neil Thomas	Senior Lecturer in Social Administration at Birmingham University. During the early 1970s he spent some years providing courses for senior and middle managers in the re-organised Social Work and Social Services Departments. He has undertaken a wide range of research projects for central and local government examining the delivery of social care. He is currently directing a study of Community Service Orders commissioned by the Home Office and he edits the Clearing House for Social Service Research.
Drew Reith	Divisional Director in the South Wales/South West England Division of Barnardo's. He was previously Unit Organiser of the Edinburgh Family Service Unit. He is the author of several articles on social work with families and the organisation of social service agencies.
Brian Sheldon	At present a lecturer in Psychology and Social Work at the University of Birmingham, though he is soon to take up the post of Director of Applied Social Studies Courses, Bedford and Royal Holloway Colleges, University of London. His main interests are social work evaluation and research and behaviour modification.
Alison Wallace	Graduated in Sociology in 1976. She worked as a researcher in the Department of Social Work, Aberdeen University for two years, and co-authored the book 'Verdicts on Social Work' with Stuart Rees. In 1981 she worked in the Social Work Department of Sydney University evaluating and monitoring students' responses to a new course. She is currently employed as a research officer in the New South Wales Bureau of Crime Statistics and Research, working on projects concerned with domestic violence, sexual assault and homicide.

Stuart Rees	Professor of Social Work at the University of Sydney. He previously worked for several years in probation and community work in England and Canada and has taught in universities in the U.S.A., Canada and Scotland. Between 1969 and 1978 he was lecturer and Senior Lecturer in Social Work in the University of Aberdeen. His other publications include: 'Social Work Face to Face' (Arnold 1978) and, with Alison Wallace 'Verdicts on Social Work' (Arnold 1982). Another client evaluation study, 'Disabled Children, Disabling Policies' was published in 1984.
Maureen Buist	Senior Research Officer in School of Social Administration, Dundee University. Research interests in educational and social aspects of disadvantaged children, and include studies of interdisciplinary assessment, home and school situation, children after a period of residential care, and the role of guidance and remedial teachers in relation to socially vulnerable children.
David Challis	Qualified in social work at Manchester University and has worked as a social worker in a mental health department, area team and hospital settings in both Lancashire and Salford. He is at present Research Fellow in the Personal Social Services Research Unit at the University of Kent. Most recently has been working with Bleddyn Davies on a study of the costs of and effectiveness of a scheme for improving care at home for the frail elderly, and on a study of the field organisation of social work.
Bleddyn Davies	Professor of Social Policy and Director of the PSSRU at the University of Kent. He has written a number of works on various aspects of social policy including one with Martin Knapp on the promotion of quality of life in Old People's Homes. Recently he has been working with David Challis on a study of the costs and effectiveness of a scheme for improving care at home for the elderly.
Martin Knapp	Lecturer in Economics at the University of Kent at Canterbury and a Research Fellow in the Personal Social Services Research Unit. He has published a book on 'The Economics of Social Care' and his current research activities include work on child care services and intermediate treatment.

Gilbert Smith	Professor and Head of the Department of Social Administration, University of Hull. He was previously Research Fellow at the Institute of Medical Sociology, Aberdeen University, a research adviser in the Scottish Office and then Reader in Social Administration and Social Work at Glasgow University. His publications include 'Social Need: Policy, Practice and Research' (R.K.P. 1980).
Caroline Cantley	Research Assistant, Department of Community Medicine, Aberdeen University, currently engaged on a study of patterns and pathways in the care of the elderly. Previously Research Assistant in the Department of Social Administration and Social Work, Glasgow University. She is a qualified social worker. Publications stemming from her research work include articles in the British Journal of Social Work and Ageing and Society.
John Tibbitt	Principal Research Officer in the Central Research Unit of the Scottish Office attached to Social Work Services Group in the Scottish Education Department. Prior to taking up his present post he conducted research for a Local Authority Social Services Department. He is author of 'Social Workers as Mental Health Officers' HMSO, 1978 and 'Health and Personal Social Services in the U.K.: Inter-Organisation Behaviour and Service Development' in Williamson, A. & Room, G. (Eds.) Welfare States in Britain. London, Heinemann.

Preface to the Second Edition

Joyce Lishman

The first edition of Evaluation was published in 1984. Since then evaluation of social work and the social services has become increasingly important. While 'practitioners, managers and service providers' still 'increasingly recognise the need to evaluate their work' evaluation is also part of the political agenda, with growing external demand for evidence of effectiveness and 'value for money'. If social workers and service providers fail to evaluate their own work external appraisal is likely to be imposed.

The second edition of this volume updates the text and references for many chapters, while others remain unchanged. Although there have been various developments in the four years since publication of the first edition, notably in the areas of quality assurance and performance review, the issues remain the same, and the collection continues to be both timely and needed. However, another four years may well see changes fundamental enough to justify a completely new collection addressing developments in the evaluation of social work and social services since 1984.

Editorial

Joyce Lishman

Although the gap between research and practice continues, practitioners, managers and service providers increasingly recognise the need to evaluate their work. Nevertheless the newcomer to evaluation research, however willing, is rightly apprehensive. He faces a bewildering array of problems inherent in both the methodology of evaluation and its application to the social services. As Thomas points out, the lack of a definitive formulation to any social problem, the centrality of political and value considerations and the inter-relatedness both of social problems and the services intended to ameliorate them complicate the task of evaluation since aims, inputs and outcome may be unclear.

This volume aims to answer the question 'What can research tell a planner, manager or practitioner, who wishes to evaluate a service, project or piece of work about methods of evaluation in general, and which method might be most appropriate for this specific task?' Each chapter explores one approach; the implications for its use; the advantages, disadvantages and limitations; and its appropriateness for evaluating what kind of work.

The approaches discussed range from quantitative to qualitative and the scale from single cases to overall service provision. Reith and Sheldon present methods appropriate for the individual practitioner evaluating his own work, both qualitative e.g. descriptive case studies and quantitative e.g. single-case evaluation designs. Both authors show how this kind of research can be an integral part of practice.

Subsequent chapters address evaluation on a larger scale, ranging from studies of a few clients or workers engaged in a particular activity to those of the development of a new service or comparing different types of service provision.

Sheldon and Challis et al explore a quantitative approach. Challis et al describe cost-effectiveness analysis, arguing that any decision to implement one kind of service involves an opportunity cost of another foregone: the more explicit we are about comparing the opportunity costs of what we provide, the clearer are the value judgements involved in the decision making. Sheldon argues for experimental methods as the strictest test of the effectiveness of what we do. While the need to specify clear goals entails a risk of failure, the resultant identification of conditions for failure or success increases our understanding of effective intervention.

Buist, and Wallace and Rees explore a qualitative approach. Buist describes the development of illuminative methods in education research as a result of dissatisfaction with the limitations of both traditional experimental and qualitative design. Wallace and Rees argue for the primacy of clients' evaluations: the social services must be accountable to the consumer.

Although quantitative and qualitative methods may at first sight appear incompatible, several contributors stress the need for combined approaches to evaluation e.g. experimental methods focussing on the achievement of specific goals can be combined with qualitative studies of consumer satisfaction.

Smith and Cantley suggest a pluralistic model combining a variety of qualitative indications (particularly the perceptions of all participants) with appropriate hard data. The question is not whether a service is globally successful, but what parts of the service are or are not successful in what ways according to whom.

A similar rephrasing might be applied to the question 'How far does this volume achieve its aims?'.

Evaluative Research and the Personal Social Services

Neil Thomas

> 'An essential attribute of any profession is that its members are active in creating and extending its knowledge, the theoretical bases for its practice and the means by which it is evaluated ... Given the complexity of so many of the problems encountered by social workers, and current uncertainty about the appropriateness and effectiveness of different modes of intervention, the lack of commitment to research is especially disturbing' [1].

This quotation is taken from the conclusions of a report on the relationship between research and practice in the personal social services, which also concluded that 'teachers in social work education have made a disappointingly limited contribution to the advancement through research of our understanding of the personal social services, in general, and of the practice of social work, in particular'. It speculated that the reasons for this sorry state of affairs might include the temperament, education and experience of social workers and social work teachers; the focus upon the unique needs of clients as opposed to the supposed detachment and categorisation involved in research; the anti-intellectual nature of some social work courses; the work patterns of social work teachers which have their roots in individualised models of practice; a belief that the skills needed for research are wholly different from those needed for practice; and a lack of opportunity to acquire those skills.

Although social workers only constitute about one in ten of the employees of a social services department, they have a major role in translating people's 'problems' into 'needs' for a wide variety of services, and many important decisions on the allocation of resources are made by managers drawn from their ranks. They undergo a longer period of education and training than many other social service employees. If their attitude to research is equivocal, it can hardly surprise us when home help organisers, day centre managers or heads of residential homes lack the confidence and enthusiasm to utilise and contribute to research.

Yet other forces have pulled in a different direction. The research sections which grew like mushrooms in social services and (to a lesser extent) social work departments after 1971 have, for the most part, taken firm root [2]. The research carried out has moved on from simplistic surveys of needs to a more sophisticated range of work, which is likely to encompass complex service planning, development and evaluation and in which user opinion is becoming more prominent [3] [4]. There has also been a burgeoning of research funded by central government. To date, much of this work has focussed upon social service, rather than social work per se. However, we do have studies which have monitored the activities of area teams [5] [6] and particular aspects of social work practice have been evaluated by Gibbons [7], Tizard [8], Fisher, Newton and Sainsbury [9] and Rees [10] among others. Increasingly practitioners have been involved in research, not least in the preparation of dissertations for Masters degree courses.

The demand for more cost-effective services in the face of expenditure restrictions has also led to a greater demand for evaluation, even if these analyses have sometimes been undertaken quickly, based upon inadequate evidence and with more attention paid to costs than effectiveness.

Attacks upon the efficacy of existing services have brought further pressure. It may be possible to discount the work of Brewer and Lait [11] as an unscholarly polemic, and to assert that Hadley and Hatch [12] have been too sweeping in their criticisms, but it is less easy to refute the plethora of studies casting doubt upon some social work practice in relation to juvenile justice [13] [14]. Similarly Davies' [15] comments on the inefficient ways in which we deliver community support to old people must be respected, given the detailed studies in which he has been involved.

This overall picture is confused, with two broad trends moving in different directions, yet the combination of these trends spells danger for social work. If the dominant professional group in the personal social services fails to involve itself in evaluative research and fails to become an active and critical consumer of it, the likely consequences are that many of the prescriptions for practice derived from sound research will go unheeded. We will not provide recipients with as much help as we could and in some instances we will harm them. At the same time others will continue to examine services made vulnerable to attack by the profession's neglect of evaluation, and the profession will have limited power – and right – to resist externally imposed solutions, based upon inadequate evidence and argument.

There are, however, inherent difficulties in evaluative research which are exacerbated by the functions of the personal social services within the broad network of social welfare provision. The following definition of evaluation highlights the problems; Suchman [16] defines it as a 'method of determining the degree to which a planned programme achieves the desired objective. Evaluative research asks about the kinds of change desired, the means by which this change is to be brought about and the signs according to which such change can be recognised'.

Goldberg and Connelly [3], on whom this discussion draws in part, point out that this implies clarity about the aims pursued, the needs to be met, the means by which this is done and the criteria against which outcome can be measured. They note that these conditions are frequently not met. Aims are often not explicit; they may be multiple and may sometimes conflict, without any clear priority being stated and the individuals concerned may not share the same aims – providers and consumers, for example. Needs, in so far as they are defined, may be viewed differently, depending on whether one's perspective is that of the consumer, the expert undertaking a systematic assessment of functioning, or the administrator concerned with eligibility and rationing of services. Given the wide spectrum of services and other help which may be directed at a person or problem, it is often difficult adequately to describe that help, let alone trace the relationships between inputs and outcomes, although the more specific and self-contained the service, the easier it will be (which may explain why studies of residential care have often been so fruitful). But evaluation of a defined self-contained service with specified inputs is not the norm: evaluations of broad programmes with multiple inputs are more likely to be required. Similarly problems of definition arise in the measurement of outcome: measurement implies specification, which diffuse multiple objectives are unlikely to yield. Whose perspective(s) do we take in this, over what period of time?

A final complication, omitted by Suchman [16] relates to the measurement of costs. Here an adequate assessment would need to include the financial, social and opportunity costs falling upon various parties, including recipients and informal carers.

We can reasonably hope that, as evaluative research develops, technical progress will be made towards meeting some of these problems and this volume points to a number of directions forward. However, certain difficulties are likely to prove intractable. These relate to the very nature of social problems as well as to the place of the personal social services in meeting them.

SOCIAL PROBLEMS AND THE PERSONAL SOCIAL SERVICES

Social problems have often been characterised as 'wicked'. The conflicts over the nature of deprivation and how it might be countered illustrate how there is no definition and how it might be countered illustrate how there is no definitive formulation of any social problem. Nor, therefore, is there a finite range of explanations, let alone solutions, which can be drawn up. The testing of any solutions must be imperfect, since cause and effect relationships are obscure and unintended consequences may only be attributed (controversially) with hindsight. Political and value considerations are central. Solutions are not seen just as proven or unproven: they are 'good' and 'bad', but from whose point of view? A further political consideration intrudes: in the natural sciences, refutation is central and negative results are considered valuable, but in social provision the instigators of a failed experiment may pay a high price. There is thus little encouragement to expose failures and allow others to learn from them. The nature of the personal social services compounds these difficulties [17]:

> 'The administrative unity of local authority personal social services departments encompasses a great variety of functions, directed towards a heterogeneous range of needs and draws upon a highly complex division of skills. They are, par excellence, a labour intensive service. Effectiveness in the field of social care is contingent on co-operation with other agencies across administrative boundaries, involving central as well as other local authority departments'.

The focus is upon 'people who are either physically or emotionally vulnerable, deprived, disturbed, deviant or destructive' [18] and some of the solutions to their difficulties – if not the difficulties themselves – lie in their relationships with other social services. The Seebohm Report [19] spoke of adequate housing as one of the foundations of an effective family service, yet we know that children, old people and mentally disordered people still come into residential care because they lack it. Similarly the need for social care among the physically handicapped or frail would be much reduced if their accommodation fitted their needs.

Poverty lies at the heart of many of the problems with which the personal social services are asked to deal. We can infer, too, that large scale unemployment, including the mass redundancy of the late middle aged, is bound to have both an immediate and long term effect on the demand for social care – and perhaps its supply – even if there is little conclusive research evidence on the matter.

The catalogue of inter-relationships is, of course, lengthy. It includes the health and social care of vulnerable groups; the social origins of illness [20]: the link between school organisation, school refusal and services for youngsters in trouble [21]; and relationships with the legal system and quasi-judicial bodies such as tribunals [22].

As if these complexities were not enough, the mixed economy of social care, in which informal support, voluntary help, statutory provision and commercial activity sometimes 'intermingle' [23] to good effect, but more often do not, adds a further set of inter-relationships.

THE ORGANISATION OF RESEARCH

The narrow organisational base of research (within social services or social work departments or sponsored by central government with a similar service focus) tends to result in the neglect of many of these complexities.

The starting point is usually from the operations of the departments. Samples are drawn from users of services, rather than non-users, thus ignoring issues such as what distinguishes one group from another. The focus is often upon the development of services within each department's own ambit, rather than any alternative solutions provided by others.

Even when the funding base is not so restrictive it is difficult to gain access to a wider range of people willing to act as research subjects. Recipients of services provide a more captive audience and the administrative records an easy source of data, so the temptations to retain a narrow focus are considerable.

Research linked to joint planning between health, social services and, perhaps, housing has improved matters [24] [25]. Yet few, if any, studies encompass the full range of services which can act as substitutes for, complements to or competitors with each other in the broad field of social care. Who gets what and in what combinations? What gaps exist? Are some services stigmatising alternatives for those of lowest social status? Plank's work on the elderly [26] is wider than most and his conclusions were more disturbing than most. It is, perhaps, significant that he worked under the aegis of the G.L.C. Central Research Unit.

WHAT SORT OF RESEARCH

We are faced with a complex, sometimes intractable, array of problems in response to which our research effort to date has been patchy. In some areas considerable progress has been made: in many others it is underdeveloped, to say the least. Basic descriptive and conceptual work still remains to be done before evaluation can take place.

To apply the normal tenets of scientific evaluation to this preparadigmatic state of affairs (see Sheldon in this volume) is to court disaster. Reid quoted in Goldberg and Connelly [3] has described some of the early American studies as 'bad marriages between tight design and loose programmes' for precisely this reason. Given that we have to apply a variety of research methods to a complex range of services, some categorisation may help the discussion. The framework chosen here is a combination of two different approaches used by Goldberg and her collaborators [3] [27].

Type of Research	Focus of Research	Problems	Becoming a Client	Providing Help	Out-comes
Description					
Monitoring					
Consumer Views					
Experiments					
Quasi-experiments					
Cross-sectional Designs					

A first use of the matrix is to highlight the fact that some of the categories within it make little sense. It is hard to conceive of an experiment which does not focus primarily upon outcomes, even if careful descriptions of the earlier stages of the process of social care form part of the research. Similarly the validity of a purely descriptive study which purported to examine outcomes would rightly be questioned. Space does not permit an exhaustive discussion of each type and focus of research, but it is important to emphasise a number of issues which arise.

First, there is still considerable scope for sensitive descriptions of the problems which people face, the processes which lead them to become clients and the services provided. These accounts will be enriched if they can be linked to broader theories and concepts.

Goffman's seminal work on asylums [28] and stigma [29] owed as much to his critical imagination as to his empirical work.

Pinker [17] argues that we suffer from a lack of adequate concepts and consequently a lack of theoretical content. He discusses the difficulties of constructing a model of social care which describes the key characteristics of the personal social services and relates them to changing family and community structures, attitudes towards dependency, rights of privacy, reciprocity and informality and the distribution of costs and benefits.

Progress has been made on a less ambitious scale. Bayley has attempted to utilise his descriptive analysis of the relationship between formal, informal and family help for mentally handicapped people [23] in the design of other schemes [30]. Abrams et al [31] have drawn on the sociological literature about localities in their analysis of good neighbour schemes. Leat [32] has moved from description to conceptualisation in her work on voluntary help.

A more purposive use of descriptive and analytical models is also beginning to occur. The Child Care Research Unit at Bradford [33] constructed a descriptive model of the system for children in trouble, which enabled them to predict future trends. Furthermore, several models have been used to describe and evaluate residential institutions [34]. More recently, Davies and his colleagues have been using an economic ('production relations') model as the basis for their evaluations of the cost-effectiveness of various provisions for the elderly [35] (see Challis et al in this volume).

However, we frequently fail to use and build upon the concepts which have been developed. For example, many surveys of the elderly work through an initial liturgy of questions about age, sex, marital status, dependency, household composition and so on, without attempting to make use of them as major elements in their subsequent analysis, despite the extensive literature on scales of, for example, dependency, social isolation and attitudes [36]. Equally, the work of Isaacs et al [37] on the reasons why family support is limited for some old people goes largely ignored.

A particularly fruitful, but neglected, area of descriptive research is the study of problems people face before they become clients.

Unemployment, family dissolution and families containing someone who is becoming frail are cases in point. How do these individuals and families cope? To whom do they turn and with what consequences? Such studies might give us some better clues about the links between informal and formal care and between the various formal agencies. As a result we might, for example, pay more attention to particular warning signs or know better how to provide help which is less stigmatising and is given before problems have become intractable. Brown and Harris [20] found that families would endure severe distress before they asked for help which they considered stigmatising. We lack similar studies of other client groups. Goldberg et al [27] have called for studies through time of groups who possess certain characteristics or are undergoing certain experiences which will lead some of them to use the personal social services.

The notion of studies over time brings us on to monitoring. A big drawback of many description surveys is that they are snapshots. They may try to explore what went before, but they cannot predict subsequent events. As Goldberg [38] illustrates, a system which traces client characteristics, problems addressed and service interventions over time, brings us nearer to evaluation, particularly if aims can also be specified. We can then paint a clearer picture of what departments are doing, or attempting to do, and who gets what. We can also find clues to questions such as 'do those who get less or different services keep coming back and demand more in the long run?'

And while such systems cannot provide answers about effectiveness, they can act as a very useful sample frame, by which small groups with particular problems or receiving particular services can be identified for detailed evaluative study. Some of the psychiatric case registers have been used in this way [39].

Goldberg and Connelly [3] also commend the combination of such monitoring with consumer research. Consumer research is discussed by Rees and Wallace in this volume, so that only one aspect will be covered here: the definition of 'consumers'.

Even if we set aside the view of several commentators that the state is the ultimate consumer through the encouragement of social order, Smith and Cantley in this volume and Allen elsewhere [40] demonstrate that the matter is by no means simple. Allen examined the impact of short term residential care for old people on the recipients of that care, their relatives, the staff and permanent residents of any long-stay homes that were used for this purpose. It was a lifeline to the primary carers. It was strongly criticised by the other groups except where it took place in homes set aside primarily for short-term care. Somewhat similar findings can be found among studies of the mentally disordered, where the recipient of care may suffer to the benefit of other members of his or her family.

Furthermore, as Smith and Cantley demonstrate, professionals from other services or sections of the same service may be important beneficiaries. Pinker [17] argues that the development of the personal social services has enabled the medical profession to export some of these patients with the worst prognosis and lowest status. Similarly, assessment centres for children are often seen to suffer in order that other aspects of care might be protected.

One way out of this dilemma is to assert, with Wallace and Rees, that client opinion should take precedence. That may be, and the past neglect of consumer studies is only belatedly being rectified [41]. Yet the researcher who is concerned to improve services will ignore such benefits to other providers at his peril. The organisational literature is replete with examples of 'dynamic conservatism' [42] by which providers resisted changes which went against their interests.

The complexities of consumer research also have implications for the choice of research methods. If 'competing accounts' are likely to exist among the various parties (see Smith and Cantley) it is valuable to augment these with observation and with analysis of written data. Of course the observation will only provide another subjective account – that of the researcher – and the records and other written data will partly reflect the writers' view of the world. But at least such methods may increase the probability of corroborating (or not) some of the accounts proferred.

Experimental designs, where members of the target group are assigned on a random or matched basis to sub-groups receiving different services and the outcome is assessed by an evaluator who is ignorant of this assignment, are dealt with in this volume by Sheldon. So, too, are quasi-experiments, in which control or comparison groups are drawn from socially similar populations living elsewhere, in the hope that this difference will not introduce variables which are not controlled.

A number of problems may arise with such studies. While those providing the experimental service may be sufficiently committed to the research to resist changes in practice when they learn from their mistakes, those providing the control service are unlikely to share that commitment, so that the service being compared is not held constant. In particular, their ideas are likely to be 'contaminated' by contact with workers from the experimental service. Again, random assignment may be resisted or even sabotaged by practitioners who do not believe that certain new approaches should be witheld from potential beneficiaries. The time which such experiments take increases the risk that unexpected events will disrupt the services provided. Finally, experiments may show that certain interventions bring results, but they cannot say why this occurs. Particularly in small scale experiments, with one or two practitioners involved, any change may be more to do with the practitioner than with the method.

For such reasons Sinclair and Clarke [43] have argued their preference for cross-sectional designs (they call them 'cross institutional comparison'). Here the outcomes of a variety of naturally different services are compared, such as differing regimes in residential institutions for similar clients. Then the sources of difference are explored to try to explain why different results were found. Of course, one requires sensitive measures of differences among recipients and service inputs and one can never be sure that the measures are sufficient, just as one can only hope to control all the relevant variables in an experiment. Equally, the correlation techniques used in such studies cannot relate cause to effect. Reasonable measures of outcome are also required. Nevertheless, studies of this sort – particularly if samples are derived from monitoring schemes from which we know something of who has received what and for how long – may help us to determine what seems to work better, for whom, and under which conditions.

Both these comparative studies and the experimental ones mentioned earlier demand careful, detailed work, focussing on small-scale service provision. They often require several years to complete, some of which time will be spent in the development of quite complex measures, say, of the impact of that service upon a recipient's social functioning. The danger is that they will find themselves reporting on yesterday's solution if not yesterday's problem. Klein [24] argues that these approaches can best be developed if research units are funded to refine their methods over a series of studies. The fruits may be seen, for example, in the work of Dartington Research Unit [44] and some of the Home Office Research Unit's studies. The investment in the Personal Social Services Research Unit at the University of Kent also holds out a promise of rich returns.

At the other extreme – and at the same time – Klein [45] notes that a very different type of evaluation needs to go on. It concerns the critical questioning of broad policy issues. An obvious current example is the duty of families to care for their members and the supporting provision which they have a right to expect. Another would be the extent to which current social policies towards the elderly force them into a state of dependency, as Townsend [46] suggests. We have seen that there can be many competing formulations of these problems and even more competing solutions, all of which are likely to have unintended consequences. Empirical research cannot provide definitive evidence upon which to base value choices about competing problem formulations and solutions. The selection of the research problem itself reflects a value choice.

There is, clearly, a link between these two types of evaluation: a particular service being evaluated does, after all, represent one solution to a problem defined in a certain way. Yet in scope and style they are a very long way apart. We can only conclude, with Klein, that both types of work are necessary, that they fit together uncomfortably and that there needs to be a continuing dialectic between the two.

CONCLUSION

Given the richness and variety of the subject matter of social services research and of the methods available for it, detailed prescription is impossible. Later contributors go on to examine particular aspects of evaluation in some detail. The strong plea that should be made at this point is that it is dangerous to move towards evaluative research designs at too early a stage. By their nature they have to be closely defined. In many of the areas with which social work and social services are concerned we know too little to construe matters in this way. Critical thought, sensitive description and attention to competing viewpoints will often have to come first. There is scope for many people – not just professional research workers – in this difficult, messy and exciting task.

References

1. CCETSW/PSSC. Research and Practice. Report of a Working Party on a Research Strategy for the Personal Social Services. CCETSW, London, 1980.
2. Bowl, R. & Fuller, R.A Study of Research in Social Services and Social Work Departments, University of Birmingham, 1982.
3. Goldberg, E.M. & Connelly, N. The Effectiveness of Social Care for the Elderly. Heinemann, London, 1982.
4. Clearing House for Social Services Research. Department of Social Administration, University of Birmingham, periodical.
5. Goldberg, E.M. & Warburton, R.W. Ends and Means in Social Work. Allen and Unwin, London, 1979.
6. Black, J., Bowl, R., Burns, D., Critcher, C., Grant, G. & Stockford, R. Social Work in Context. Tavistock, London, 1983.
7. Gibbons, J.S., Bow, I., Butler, J. & Powell, J. 'Clients' reactions to task-centred case-work: a follow-up study' British Journal of Social Work. 9. 1979, 203-15.
8. Tizard, B. Adoption: A Second Chance. Open Books, London, 1977.
9. Fisher, M., Newton, C. & Sainsbury, E. Social work support to people suffering mental ill-health and to their families. University of Sheffield, Department of Sociological Studies, 1981.
10. Rees, S. Social Work Face to Face. Edward Arnold, London, 1978.
11. Brewer, C. & Lait, J. Can Social Work Survive? Temple Smith, London, 1980.
12. Hadley, R. & Hatch, S. Social Welfare and the Failure of the State. Allen and Unwin, London, 1981.
13. Thorpe, D., Dunsby, E. & Green, C. 'Services received by juvenile offenders subject to Care Orders' in Children and Young Persons Act 1969. B.A.S.W., Birmingham, 1978.

14. Cawson, P. Young Offenders in Care: Preliminary Report. D.H.S.S., London, 1978.

15. Davies, B.P. 'Strategic goals and piecemeal innovations: adjusting to the new balance of needs and resources' In Goldberg, E.M. & Hatch, S. (Eds.). A New Look at the Personal Social Services. Policy Studies Institute, London, 1981.

16. Suchman, E.A. Evaluative Research. Russell Sage Foundation, New York, 1967.

17. Pinker, R.A. Research Priorities in the Personal Social Services. Social Science Research Council, London, 1978.

18. Jordan, B. 'A Service with a Human Face' Community Care. 6 April, 1977.

19. Report of the (Seebohm) Committee on Local Authority and Allied Personal Social Services. HMSO, London, 1968.

20. Brown, G.W. & Harris, T. Social Origins of Depression. Tavistock, London, 1978.

21. Rose, G. & Marshall, T. Counselling and School Social Work: An Experimental Study. Wiley, London, 1974.

22. Bell, K. Research study on supplementary benefit appeal tribunals. HMSO, London, 1975.

23. Bayley, M.J. Mental Handicap and Community Care. Routledge & Kegan Paul, London, 1973.

24. Mitchell, S. & Woodthorpe, J. 'A Survey of Young Mentally Handicapped People in the London Borough of Hammersmith and Fulham' Clearing House for Local Authority Social Services Research. University of Birmingham, No. 6, 1980.

25. Stockport Metropolitan Borough. The Elderly: Research and Policy Reports. Stockport, 1976.

26. Plank, D. Caring for the Elderly. Research memorandum 512, Greater London Council, London, 1977.

27. Goldberg, E.M. et al 'Report to the DHSS Research Liaison Group for Local Authority Social Services: Directions for Research in Social Work and the Social Services' British Journal of Social Work. 10, 2, 1980.

28. Goffman, E. Asylums. Anchor Books, 1961.

29. Goffman, E. Stigma: Notes on the Management of Spoiled Identity. Prentice Hall, 1968.

30. Bayley, M., Parker, P., Seyd, R. & Tennant, A. Neighbourhood Services Project-Dinnington. Paper No. 1. University of Sheffield, 1981.

31. Abrams, P., Abrams, S., Humphrey, R. & Smaith, R. Action for Care: A Review of Good Neighbour Schemes in England. Volunteer Centre, Berkhamsted, 1981.

32. Leat, D. Towards a Definition of Volunteer Involvement. Volunteer Centre, London, 1977.

33. Bradford, M.D.C. Social Services Department. 'Working Paper Describing Possible Approaches to Modelling the Child Care Placement System' Clearing House for Social Services Research. University of Birmingham, No. 1, 1980.

34. Miller, E.J. & Gwynne, G.V. A Life Apart. Tavistock, London, 1972.

35. For example, Davies, B. & Knapp, M. Old People's Homes and the Production of Welfare. Routledge & Kegan Paul, London, 1980.

36. Abrams, M. People in their Late Sixties: A Longitudinal Survey of Ageing. Age Concern Research Unit, Mitcham, 1983.

37. Isaacs, B., Livingstone, M. & Neville, Y. The Survival of the Unfittest. Routledge and Kegan Paul, London, 1972.

38. Goldberg, E.M. 'Monitoring in the Social Services' In Goldberg, E.M. & Connelly, N. (Eds.) Evaluative Research in Social Care. Heinemann, London, 1981.

39. Wing, J. 'Monitoring in the Field of Psychiatry' In Goldberg, E.M. & Connelly, N. (Eds.) Evaluative Research in Social Care. Heinemann, London, 1981.

40. Allen, I. Short-Stay Residential Care for the Elderly. Policy Studies Institute, London, 1982.

41. For example, Clearing House for Local Authority Social Services Research. No. 7, 1983 included local consumer studies of assisted lodgings for the elderly (Birmingham), facilities for visitors to a long-stay hospital (West Sussex) and a home care worker scheme (Westminister).

42. Schon, D. Beyond the Stable State. Temple Smith, London, 1971.

43. Sinclair, I. & Clarke, R. 'Cross-institutional Designs' In Goldberg, E.M. & Connelly, N. (Eds.) Evaluative Research in social Care. Heinemann, London, 1981.

44. Millham, S., Bullock, R. & Cherrett, P. After Grace, Teeth. Human Context Books, London, 1975.

45. Klein, R. The Evaluation of Social Policies. (mimeo) Bath, 1981.

46. Townsend, P. 'The Structured Dependency of the Elderly: Creation of Social Policy in the Twentieth Century' Ageing and Society. 1, 1, March, 1981.

Evaluation - a Function of Practice

Drew Reith

Social workers need to take action themselves to gain and to demonstrate greater confidence and certainty in the effectiveness of their activities. While we have not yet recovered fully from the body-blows delivered by the succession of 'not proven' verdicts pronounced upon our effectiveness during the late sixties and early seventies [1], we now recognise some of the flaws of these early studies (such as the undifferentiated 'black box' definition of casework, and the social worker's goals of intervention being reformulated by the researcher). More positively, a number of studies carried out in the U.S. throughout the seventies have indicated that certain approaches can be effective in certain situations. Having reviewed all the controlled experimental studies of direct social work in the United States and Canada from 1973 to 1979, Reid and Hanrahan concluded that 'structured approaches addressed to specific problems, behaviours or social skills appear able to affect constructive changes'; though they go on to qualify even this cautious statement by adding the rider that 'the practical importance and durability of such changes have yet to be fully demonstrated' [2].

In order that the worth and effectiveness of social work may be established beyond reasonable doubt, social workers must start to pay more serious attention than hitherto to the findings of research and evaluative studies. Reid and Hanrahan found that the more successful interventions (and also the successful evaluations) were those which have been informed by the findings of previous experimental tests. The implication is unmistakable: we should build our practice and our means of evaluating it upon what others have tested before us and found to work, rather than relying solely on our native wit and intuition. Failure to do so leaves us continuing to operate with assumptions and methods which lack empirical validation.

It is self-evident that practice should be based on the accumulated testing and evaluating of practice, but the careful evaluations required to establish a sure foundation for practice are still few in number. One remedy, advocated strongly in this country by Sheldon, is that 'social workers should build simple evaluation devices into their work' [3].

Not that this is a new idea. Monitoring and evaluating the outcome of intervention was reckoned by a CCETSW working group on education and training for social work, to be one of the seven major functions common to all social work practice. In order to monitor the outcomes of his interventions – according to this group – the social worker 'must appreciate the potential value of records and use them for developmental as well as routine (ad hoc) purposes. He should be aware of the need to record the alternatives considered or available as well as the chosen method(s) of intervention. He must learn to devise and maintain a system of periodic review and re-assessment aimed at identifying both the developments taking place and the methods by which objectives appear to have been reached. He must critically evaluate his own intervention, and that of others. He should be capable of articulating what has been said and done and why, not only in descriptive but also conceptual terms. He must learn to put forward conclusions about the effectiveness and appropriateness of alternative methods of interventions' [4].

Most social workers and social service managers would readily accept a professional obligation to strive constantly to improve services in general and to enhance the effectiveness of their own practice in particular. Most would also agree that some form of self-evaluation is desirable. However, this has not become part of the daily routine for more than a tiny number. The time, the means, the support and perhaps the determination to incorporate evaluation into practice have not yet been found. This is not surprising in the face of institutional inertia, the daunting technical aspects, and the personal effort required. Yet it is only by reviewing and evaluating actions and activities, periodically if not continuously, that the feedback can be generated which enables assessment, planning and intervention to be modified if necessary and improved if possible. Failure to evaluate may result in unhelpful interventions being perpetrated and perpetuated without check or validation. By embracing evaluation, practice could be improved to a level well beyond that which most social workers are achieving currently.

Faintheartedness at the prospect of evaluating one's own practice is entirely understandable. Miller [5] anticipates that social workers will feel unskilled and unprepared for the task of evaluating their practice and seek to leave it to some 'expert'. She offers the following encouragement.

> 'Teachers and practitioners in social work (as in other professions and disciplines) should not begin with the idea that they are novices, to be initiated into the mysteries of evaluation research methods; they are experts

> in their own subject who, over the years, have already identified problems and processes in teaching and learning. It is this knowledge and experience which should lead to their choice of evaluation strategy – and not the other way round with the research methodology determining what can be evaluated and how'.

She argues that the experiences, values and perceptions of individual practitioners need to be much nearer to the centre of social work evaluation and research. The practitioner has an understanding of practice in his setting which far exceeds that of an external evaluator (even if that person has a background in social work).

In fact, evaluation is an activity we are performing constantly and unconsciously in our everyday lives. It involves comparing one thing with another and then making a value judgement. Most of the time we rely on commonsense, personal experience, and our own observations. Most of the time we get along tolerably well but, as Herbert [6] points out, there are hazards in relying on personal experience.

> 'The observation and recording of what is experience may be unreliable. Generalisations may be formed on the basis of inadequate evidence. Evidence may be distorted by personal biases or neglected because it does not accord with previous experience. The salient features of a situation may not be distinguished from those which were irrelevant. Causal inference may be incorrectly or prematurely drawn.'

If our commonsense, intuition and empirical reasoning are not wholly reliable in guiding our own lives and actions, far less will they be reliable as we try to help other people with theirs. The critical difference between conscious and unconscious evaluations lies in the extent to which the relevant information and the underlying assumptions and criteria are explicit and available for examination.

The purpose of evaluation is, straightforwardly, to provide feedback. Posavac and Carey note that 'human behaviour is adaptive only when people obtain feedback from the environment'; and state that 'program evaluation seeks to provide feedback in social systems' [7]. There are a number of reasons for seeking feedback, including

(i) learning whether the objectives of services have been achieved as intended and discovering whether there have been any unintended consequences;
(ii) obtaining information to improve practices and procedures and to highlight training requirements;
(iii) informing decision-making and policy-review;

(iv) meeting internal and external accountability requirements; and
(v) answering requests for information.

It would be misleading to suggest that systematic evaluation is an easy undertaking. The would-be self-evaluator will be quickly bewildered by new concepts and jargon. There is no neat definition, no standard model. In fact, Patton [8] discovered scores of definitions and numerous evaluation models. His own concern is with evaluation which has a practical application:

> 'The practice of evaluation involves the systematic collection of information about the activities, characteristics, and outcomes of programs, personnel and products for use by specific people to reduce uncertainties, improve effectiveness, and make decisions with regard to what those programs, personnel or products are doing or affecting'.

Patton reproduces the six categories of evaluations specified by the Evaluation Research Society Standards Committee:

(a) *Front-end Analysis:* These types of evaluations take place prior to installation of a programme to provide guidance in planning and implementing the programme as well as deciding whether the programme should be implemented. They analyse the context and assess the feasibility.

(b) *Evaluability Assessments:* These include activities aimed at assessing the feasibility of various evaluation approaches and methods. The scope of the evaluation, technical matters, design limitations, and cost parameters are established through evaluability assessment prior to undertaking a more formal evaluation, especially a causal evaluation of programme outcomes.

(c) *Formative Evaluations:* These are aimed at providing information for programme improvement, modification and management. They tend to focus on process, but not to the exclusion of measuring effectiveness.

(d) *Impact or Summative Evaluations:* These are aimed at determining programme results and effects, especially for the purpose of making major decisions about programme continuation, expansion, reduction and funding. Since they are carried out for the purpose of making judgements about the basic worth of a programme, they tend to focus on outcomes but evaluations of implementation are not precluded.

(e) *Programme Monitoring:* The kinds of activities involved in these evaluations vary widely from periodic checks or compliance with policy to relatively straightforward 'tracking' of services delivered and 'counting' of clients.

(f) *Evaluation of Evaluation:* (or secondary evaluation, meta-evaluation, evaluation audit): This category includes professional critiques of evaluation reports, re-analysis of data, and external reviews of internal evaluation.

The practitioner-evaluator is not trying to prove the effectiveness of social work, nor to carry out research into major social problems. His concern is with small-scale programme evaluation, namely the systematic collection and analysis of data which will provide information and insight into his own practice in order that he may improve it. The feedback generated should lead the social worker to reflect upon his practice on a more informed basis; pose questions about his effort, effectiveness and efficiency; provide encouragement for what he is doing well or well enough; and start to indicate which skills and techniques he should use and develop in which situations. Our search, therefore, is for means of evaluating practice which offer some reliability in the context and specific circumstances of our day-to-day activities.

Social work and evaluation are coming to be compatible activities. The need to design evaluations which take account of the highly individualised nature of social work has to be met. Equally, the evaluation requirement that the goals and techniques of social work intervention should be expressed in specific, explicit and unambiguous terms is now inherent in a number of social work methods.

The following section describes some of the ways by which social workers might evaluate their own practice.

APPROACHES

Periodic and Termination Evaluation

As noted earlier, review and evaluation of work are to be regarded as part of the social worker's standard practice, taking place at regular intervals and at the point of terminating the work. The more specific the goals and the more clearly baseline information can be established, the easier it is subsequently to judge the extent to which goals have been realised. Careful recording of progress is essential, as are sessions in which the social worker and client check out their perceptions of what is taking place. It hardly requires repeating that behavioural approaches are well suited for evaluation since they incorporate establishing baseline behaviours, monitoring progress and measuring case outcomes.

Evaluation as Part of the Practice Method

The procedure in which practice and evaluation are most closely combined is the experimental investigation of single cases. Since this approach is the subject of a later chapter, it will suffice here to state that this method, once grasped, can be undertaken readily by practitioners, can be introduced by the individual into his practice without major disruption to clients or agency, and produces information which should improve the service to clients and the knowledge and skills of the worker.

Other less rigorous quasi-experimental approaches have been described by Fischer [9]. The 'objectified case study', like the single case design, emphasises 'systematic, planned interventions and careful recording of effects in an effort to isolate the specific techniques that are related to specific changes in problem behaviours'. It attempts to relate the processes and techniques of intervention (which are varied systematically) to the outcomes of the intervention. However, because the methods are less rigorous, conclusions are more tentative.

The 'measurement model' is the name coined for a series of short, easily administered instruments [9] to aid in evaluating the extent of the client's problems, and to provide ongoing evaluative feedback on progress. These scales are answered by clients in a very brief time so as to be as simple and non-threatening as possible. They can be scored on the spot, and the client given instant feedback. These are information-collecting devices, rather than evaluations of outcome, but they are reported as having extensive reliability and validity. The scales are designed to be used every week or two as a measure for monitoring, assessing, and guiding the course of intervention on a continuous basis.

The 'A Priori Model' involves the determination, in advance, of the stages through which an interventive process will pass. The key ingredient is that the worker and client cannot progress from one stage to another unless certain specified criteria are met. This model is in its infancy but, when fully developed, it promises practical, outcome-orientated advantages in that criteria of success are built into each stage. It also has the potential to isolate the various elements of the process that contribute most to overall outcome.

Descriptive Case Studies

Social workers' efforts to conceptualise and develop their practice have relied heavily on descriptions of their work with individual cases (or groups, or whatever). Most of these descriptions are impressionistic; and any discussion and 'conclusions' owe as much to the worker's intuition, empathy and insight as they do to the information available.

Thomas [10] drawing on surveys of the community work literature, reports the failure of much of the case study literature to prepare any analytic frameworks or concepts from the actions described. He regrets this failure because 'case studies are a useful means to develop theories out of the "home-grown" practice of community workers'. He suggests some broad questions which might generally be expected to be addressed in a community work case study. His further remarks are readily translatable into other settings:

> 'For the purpose of studying practice it is essential that the role and activity of the worker and the assumptions and thinking on which these are based should be given as much attention as the work of the target group or organisation and the development of the interaction. This should include also a critical appraisal by the worker of his or her own approach and actions.
>
> Ideally, the case study should include enough information to enable the reader to make his or her own interpretation of the situation. Such a mixture of descriptive and analytic material would also provide a basis for more general propositions or hypotheses about the practice of community work. This is a very demanding task. Potentially, however, case studies are not merely an illustration of theory developed for other purposes but an important source of an indigenous theory of practice.'

A major limitation in case studies is that information tends not to be collected systematically or rigorously, and this makes subsequent analysis haphazard. Davies [11] acknowledges that descriptive work can have a value, but expresses the hope that the literature will not continue 'to be dominated by descriptive assertions that sound like proven facts but which in truth still await empirical investigation'.

As a minimum requirement, goals need to be specific and the worker's intervention clearly identified. A recording system must then be designed which allows progress to be followed and searching questions asked. A useful illustration and discussion of this is Butler's description of her use of specific objectives and tasks in work with a family [12].

A rough and ready method of self-evaluation is proposed by Douglas and Payne [13] which requires little extra time and resources. This enables only a general picture to be drawn of a unit but it can, they claim, become the basis for a continuing assessment of its functioning. The procedures are as follows:

1. Clarify unit objectives.
2. List one or two significant steps towards each identified goal.
3. Select those activities that are intended or appear to contribute to each of the steps.
4. Record statements on a chart.
5. Rate (evaluate) each activity for its contribution, e.g. by scoring in terms of whether it makes a high, medium or low contribution.

A further approach is being developed by Miller and Sexton [14] which they call illuminative evaluation (see also Buist in this volume). The object is simply to shed light on our activities – to make them clear to other people who are not necessarily directly involved in those activities themselves. The guiding principles of illuminative evaluation are:

(i) that people do it for themselves (on the basis that participants are the people in the best position to evaluate an activity);
(ii) that the evaluation process is designed to fit the particular activity, its setting and its context; it is not imposed from outside;
(iii) that it is practical;
(iv) that it is as much concerned with answering questions thrown up by the examination of the activity as it is with applying externally derived criteria to that activity; and
(v) that it is as much concerned with making clear the processes involved in the activity as it is with attempting to measure the unknowns of that activity. The direct and indirect advantages of practitioners evaluating their own work are reported enthusiastically by the authors.

Systematised Recording

Countless attempts have been made to devise more systematic ways of recording information on the client's problems and on the process and effects of intervention. This approach, in Fischer's view [9], is also less rigorous because it relies heavily on the social worker's judgement of his own efforts, albeit supplemented perhaps with the client's reports of progress, and because it does not control the variables in a systematic way. While unequivocal proof of effectiveness is not possible, there is some evidence that such recording can produce significant gains in efficiency through eliminating the need for extensive recording. They also have the effect of orienting practitioners to outcome and to evaluating the effects of their interventions.

The task-centred approach is one example of a method which incorporates systematised planning and recording procedures. Areas typically covered in such instruments include target problems; specific objectives; time scales; workers' roles; client tasks in relation to specific objectives; worker activities; and so on [15].

Monitoring by Means of Information Systems

All agencies have some means of collecting, storing, retrieving and working data on clients, services, staff involvement and case outcomes. Few, however, seem to collect the kind of information about service processes and outcomes that would be useful to practitioners. Categories of client problems and agency responses tend to be crude, and the data elicited may not be very reliable. Designed, often as administrative information systems for establishing managerial accountability, they are not evaluative tools in themselves; but they may provide data which could assist in setting up an evaluation. Use of any information system begins by asking questions of the data: 'if you don't ask questions, you won't get answers' [8]

The best known system in the United Kingdom is the Case Review System designed by Goldberg and her colleagues [16] in collaboration with the staff of one local authority area team. This work had two aims:

(1) To develop a model information and review system which would enable fieldworkers and management to monitor their social work and social services activities in order to discover how professional skills and other social service resources are used in relation to different problems presented and to different aims pursued.

(2) To encourage social workers to become more explicit about both means and ends of their activities'.

This system deliberately set out to be practitioner-focussed rather than management-focussed, and some considerable progress was made in developing a form which gained acceptance by social workers. (It is so well documented and easily obtainable that it need not be described in detail here). In an evaluation of the system, only a proportion of the social workers expressed a commitment to the Case Review System as an aid to their individual practice (i.e. helping in setting goals and becoming more explicit about aims, in clarifying priorities, and in defining limits including time-limits). There was a much wider acceptance of it as a monitoring and planning tool which enabled them to compare their own contributions with those of their colleagues and with the work of the area office as a whole.

'There was general consensus that the presence of the research team had generated new thinking, new ideas and enthusiasm, and had contributed to the generally good morale of the area and to a sense of purpose, but the problem now was how to keep the interest going'. The two most serious general reservations expressed about the system were its cost and whether the resultant benefit justified the social workers' effort. The researchers [16] for their part had declared that 'whether the Case Review System had an impact on individual casework practices remains an open question' and speculate that an instrument designed in one setting may not be transferable 'cold' to another. The act of creating the system may be an indispensable factor in its gaining acceptance. (The social workers involved in designing the system were more enthusiastic than those who were not). Parsloe [17], in a review of workload management and case planning systems, suggests that the design of any such system or instrument reflects the values of the author and agency.

Since social work is neither a monolithic nor a static activity, there never will be a 'perfect' information system. However, within the limitations of any existing or future system, it is worthwhile for the practitioner to consider how far he can harness it to inform and improve his own practice.

Writing elsewhere about the Case Review System, Goldberg [18] suggests that:

> 'a monitoring tool which compares problems, objectives, input and outcome over time can help individual workers to evaluate their own work by observing how aims and achievements are matched and how they relate to the work undertaken. In aggregated form such a review system enables practitioners to examine their individual caseloads as a whole and may enable them to decide on priorities and allocation of time'.

Surveys of Client Opinions

Seeking the views of consumers is now well established as a means of evaluating social work intervention. Reviewing the evolution of client-based research, Phillips [19] notes a splitting into two camps: 'The qualitative, in-depth study of feelings, perceptions and attitudes via conversational and semi-structured interviews on the one hand, and the quantitative study of hard data via structured interviews and questionnaires on the other'. The self-evaluator will be concerned only with the intensive qualitative approach, not the extensive quantitative one – at least until such time as the synthesis being explored by Fisher et al [20] proves workable.

Client reactions have been collected on both the process and outcome of their contact with social services; and several studies compare the views of both the providers and receivers of the services. The general import of these is that clients report more positive reactions than negative ones. The findings of opinion surveys tend to be more flattering to social workers than do the findings of goal-directed or criteria-led evaluations.

Phillips [19] suggests two areas particularly worthy of study:

(i) client satisfaction with the worker (recognising the difficulty with client satisfaction); and, more especially,
(ii) the client's assessment of the extent to which the social worker's involvement has helped solve or ameliorate the problems identified (either at referral or during the course of social work intervention).

Opinion surveys are best carried out by personal interview (rather than postal questionnaire), using an open-ended or semi-structured questionnaire. The temptation, once this has been chosen as the method, is for the evaluator to focus his attention on the construction of a questionnaire, before or without looking at the total process. The basic steps in setting up a survey are:

1. Define the problem to be solved or decision to be made.
2. What data or information is needed in order to solve this problem or make this decision?
3. What questions need to be answered in order to obtain this data?
4. What questions should be asked in order to answer those questions?
5. What is the best way of getting those questions answered? (It may not be by survey).
6. How many people should be asked?
7. What people should be questioned?

When reflecting upon the data generated by a survey, it should not be assumed that the responses are representative or stable: people change their minds, and often quite rapidly.

Lishman [21] is one social worker who has applied this approach to her own practice. She undertook a follow-up survey of twelve of her former clients in order to explore whether clashes in perspective occur between clients and social worker, and how this is linked with satisfaction and dissatisfaction. She compared clients' reports with the records she had made at the time she was working with them.

It is evident from her presentation and discussion of the findings that she learned a great deal about her assessment of clients and her behavioural responses to them and identified a number of areas where her practice could be improved.

Parsons [22] reports on a survey he undertook of single parents who sought help from the social service team in which he was a social worker. He discusses his findings in the light of relevant literature, and poses further questions which he discusses briefly.

MANAGING EVALUATION

Planning

If evaluation is to be a worthwhile and successful undertaking it has to be planned and managed in the same way as any other part of one's workload and time. This means the practitioner organising himself and creating a climate and environment which will support his efforts.

The first and essential task is to decide the purpose of the evaluation. The purpose of the evaluation which is being contemplated needs to be worked out and written down. As suggested previously, the purpose of practitioner-evaluation is most likely to be concerned with developing the information and techniques available to enhance practice, rather than with decision-making in the organisation or with public accountability.

Once the overall purpose is clearly in view, an outline evaluation proposal needs to be composed with special attention given to framing an objective which is of manageable proportions. What is it that you are planning to do? What are you planning not to do? The more precise the stated objective, the more it will help when you begin to lose direction and feel you are sinking under the bewildering number of issues which will arise.

Some aspects of practice are more amenable to evaluation than others and there really is little point in the practitioner setting himself an impossible mission: the evaluation should satisfy the criteria of utility (i.e. making the content practical) and feasibility (i.e. making the process practical). There is no point setting out to investigate complex, obstruse constellations of issues or to discover profound truths. Seek instead to be content with a straightforward evaluation of areas closer to home. Some assessment should be made of the potential value of the evaluation, and the possible ways it could be used.

Only after the purpose, topic and objective have been clearly worked out is it safe to move on to the evaluation design. It is tempting – but it must be resisted – to rush into a design and then see what that design could provide information about.

A useful checklist is provided by Patton [8]:

What do we want to find out?

Why do we want to find that out?

When do we need the information?

How can we get the information we need?

Where should we gather information?

Who is the information for and from whom should we collect the information we need?

Organising

The evaluation proposal needs to be discussed at various stages with others who will be involved or affected – managers, colleagues, administrative and clerical staff, other agencies, and perhaps even clients. Unless they are prepared for and involved in the evaluation, more problems will arise than necessary. It is worth spending time in explaining the purpose and proposal, and in subsequently communicating progress.

Once the proposal has been worked out and agreed, thought has to be given to the technical skills and material resources which will be needed. This does not require one to take a course in research methods, but it is advisable to link up with someone who is knowledgeable in the field and can offer tuition, guidance, coaching and encouragement.

Such a consultant may be an agency's research officer or from an academic institution, where it is often possible to make informal arrangements with individual staff members. Some social work training institutions offer short (four months approximately) post-qualifying fellowships which allow practitioners to investigate a certain aspect of practice in depth. Registration for a part-time higher degree may be an answer. It is worth noting, in passing, that a number of academics have in recent years made arrangements to work in social work agencies, combining practice and evaluation.

In addition to support and supervision in the technicalities of evaluation, the practitioner who is setting out to evaluate his work needs the support of his agency, colleagues and management. Their moral support is important, as is its translation into practical help when required. Some things are best checked early, such as secretarial assistance and the availability of equipment, materials, computer time and money.

Self-direction and Motivation

The most important resource is time, but only a limited amount is available. Every effort to pace the evaluation by setting realistic tasks and targets is to be encouraged. Even if this is done, evaluation does not progress steadily and smoothly; and it always takes longer than expected because of the issues provoked by the mere act of evaluating.

During the course of carrying out an evaluation, the practitioner can expect his motivation to ebb and flow. He will question the benefit in relation to the time and energy spent. He will doubt the value and validity of his small-scale work. This is a normal part of research experience and ways have to be found of recapturing purpose and enthusiasm.

Evaluating

Some means of evaluating should be built in, in order to check that the evaluation is proceeding as intended and to provide feedback on the process. Monitoring the evaluation allows one to learn what works and what does not, and to take corrective action if necessary. It also helps in keeping expectations realistic and the expenditure of time reasonable. In the same way as evaluating practice is intended to inform and enhance practice, so monitoring and evaluating the evaluation (in however unsophisticated a way) should inform and enhance the evaluation.

The practitioner-evaluator must be prepared to be honest and open to some critical appraisals of his own competence, and to have actual or potential weaknesses exposed. In self-evaluation, one has to come to grips with some personal defences and habitual ways of going about things. When people or data are critical of us, we need to make sure we are hearing what they are saying. These are ground rules for giving and receiving feedback and these should be observed.

The evaluation and the feedback it generates has a bearing on the relationship between the practitioner as an employee and his employing agency. Evaluation of one's professional work is one of the main functions of an appraisal of one's performance as an employee. Performance appraisal is in essence an audit of how far the member of staff has accomplished his role objective and tasks according to explicit and jointly agreed standards and timescales. It would be foolish not to use the results of self-evaluation for staff development purposes, provided that the true objectives of appraisal are pursued, namely:

(i) to assess performance (recognising strengths and identifying problem areas) and to use that information to improve performance over an agreed period;
(ii) to identify areas for improvement and ways to overcome weaknesses; and
(iii) to discuss potential for development.

A strictly ethical approach is required of both the self-evaluator (not to distort findings) and the employing agency (not to misuse them). The outcome of evaluation and a proper staff appraisal could well lead to a recommendation about further training.

RECURRING ISSUES

Certain issues and topics are sure to arise in evaluating one's practice. It may be reassuring to know that they are common. Several of these were identified and reported by a group of social work teachers from both academic and practice bases who were brought together under the auspices of CCETSW to undertake collaborative research projects in practice teaching [23].

Among commonly recurring issues which emerged were the place of values in social work; the importance of being explicit about plans and intentions; the need to clarify expectations; the importance of making assumptions explicit; the need for a common language between those collaborating in the research; and the impact of the environment (e.g. conflicting demands on time).

Evaluation does take time; and we already have too little of that. It also comes up with issues which need to be dealt with – and this follow-up action also neeeds time. The hope is that the self-evaluation will lead to greater skill, and therefore to a qualitatively better and more effective service to clients.

Let us be optimistic about the possibilities for practitioner evaluation. The trend now discernible in the United States may soon have its counterpart in the United Kingdom [24]:

> 'A most important trend for the future of the practice research relationship is already underway, and that is the reduction of the sharp separation between research and practice activities. In progress now are significant efforts to merge practice and research activities. The concept of the practitioner-scientist is one symbol of that trend. This concept means not only that the same person can both practice and conduct research, but also that he or she can engage in practice and research simultaneously as a set of integrated activities. The concept makes possible an empirically based model of practice, a possibility that was inconceivable only a few years ago'.

References

1. See the review by Fischer, J. 'Is Casework Effective? A Review' in Social Work. Vol. 18, No. 1. January, 1973, 5-20.
2. Reid, W.J. & Hanrahan, P. 'The Effectiveness of Social Work: Recent Evidence' in Goldberg, E.J.M. & Connelly, N. (Eds.), Evaluative Research in Social Care. Policy Studies Institute/ Heinemann, London, 1981.
3. Sheldon, B. 'The Use of Single Case Experimental Designs in the Evaluations of Social Work' British Journal of Social Work. Vol. 13, No. 5, October, 1983, 477-500.
4. CCETSW. Education and Training for Social Work. CCETSW Paper 10, London, 1975, 27-32.
5. Miller, C. 'Evaluation Research Methods – a Guide' In Research in Practice Teaching: Papers and Projects from a Workshop. CCETSW Study 6, London, 1983, 18-26.
6. Herbert, M. 'Research: Methods of Enquiry' in CCETSW Study 6, op.cit. 27-39.
7. Posavac, E.J. & Carrey, R.G. Program Evaluation: Methods and Case Studies. Prentice-Hall, Englewood Cliffs, 1980, p. 15.
8. Patton, M.Q. Practical Evaluation. Sage Publications, Beverley Hills, 1982.

9. Fischer, J. Effective Casework Practice – An Eclectic Approach. McGraw-Hill, 1978, 102-120.
10. Thomas, D.N. The Making of Community Work. Allen and Unwin, London, 1983.
11. Davies, M. 'The Current Status of Social Work Research' British Journal of Social Work. Vol. 4, No. 3, Autumn 1974, 281-303.
12. Butler, J. 'Casework by Objectives' in Laxton, M. et al, Time to Consider. FSU/Bedford Square Press, London, 1975.
13. Douglas, R. & Payne, C. 'Home Monitors' Social Work Today. Vol. 13, No. 12, 24.11.81, p. 19.
14. Sexton, T. & Miller, C. 'Youth Work – What's it Worth?' Youth and Society. No. 87, February, 1984, 22-23.
15. See, for example, Vickery, A. Caseload Management. National Institute for Social Work, London, 1977.
16. Goldberg, E.M. & Warburton, R.W. Ends and Means in Social Work. Allen and Unwin, London, 1979, P. 21.
17. Parsloe, P. Social Services Area Teams. Allen and Unwin, London, 1981, 60-87.
18. Goldberg, E.M. 'Monitoring in the Social Services' in Goldberg, E.M. & Connelly, N. Evaluative Research in Social Care. Policy Studies Institute, 1981, 283/4.
19. Phillips, D. 'Mayer & Timms Revisited: The Evolution of Clients Studies' in Fischer, M. Speaking of Clients. Joint Unit for Social Services Research, Sheffield University, 1983, p. 8.
20. Fisher, M., Newton, C. & Sainsbury, E. Mental Health Social Work Observed. Allen and Unwin, London, 1983.
21. Lishman, J. 'A Clash in Perspective? A Study of Worker and Client Perceptions of Social Work' British Journal of Social Work. Vol. 8, No. 3, Autumn 1978, 301-311.
22. Parsons, R.J.S. 'Social Work with Single Parent Families: Consumer Views' British Journal of Social Work. Vol. 13, No. 5, October 1983, 539-558.
23. CCETSW Study 6. Teaching: Papers and Projects from a Workshop. CCETSW, London, 1983, 12-14.
24. Brian, S. 'Toward the Integration of Practice and Research' in Fanshel, D. (Ed.) Future of Social Work Research. National Association of Social Workers, Washington, 1980, p. 35.

Single Case Evaluation Methods: Review and Prospects

Brian Sheldon

THE CASE FOR A STRUCTURED APPROACH TO CASE EVALUATIONS

Anyone who digs to any depth into the pre-1974 social work effectiveness literature is likely to come across a paradoxical set of findings; favourable expectations and impressions of the participants in research programmes, and dismal final results. Several of the experimental studies [1] [2] note this phenomenon and the effect is also quite well known in psychological research [3] [4]. Here is Fischer [5] commenting on it in the Cambridge-Somerville study:

> 'Throughout the programme, counsellors were asked on several occasions to list all the treatment group boys they thought had "substantially benefitted" from the services offered by the project. Roughly two thirds of the boys were so listed. Further, at the end of treatment over half the boys volunteered that they had been helped by their caseworkers. Similarly, in a follow-up of treatment-group boys (N=254) ratings suggested that two thirds were adjusting satisfactorily ...'

The problem with these apparently reassuring findings is that no significant differences were found between experimental and control group subjects in this study!

Variations on this effect are also to be found in consumer-opinion research [6] [7] [8] where there are profound differences of interpretation between workers and clients as to what has happened, what its value is, and who is deserving of praise or blame. An analysis of reports from dissatisfied clients by Mayer and Timms concludes [6]:

> 'There is an almost Kafkaesque quality about these worker-client transactions. To exaggerate only slightly, each of the parties assumed that the other

> shared certain of his underlying conceptions about behaviour and the ways in which it might be altered. Then, unaware of the inappropriateness of his extrapolations, each found special reasons to account for the other's conduct.'

A larger, later study produced similar findings [9]:

> 'While they expressed their gratification in having the worker listen to them, they were puzzled as to how this was supposed to help. Another recurring theme was the client's expectation that the worker play a more active role in the helping process through expressed opinions, giving advice, and suggestions. This was evident among respondents from both the middle and lower socio-economic groups.'

These results, frequently repeated in consumer-studies, albeit alongside more positive outcomes, suggest that miscommunication and the misattribution of change are endemic to social work. Perhaps it would be surprising if this were not so in a profession so heavily reliant upon verbal interaction as its main medium of influence. The important questions, however, remain:

(i) how does this effect (which seems to rob social workers of accurate feedback on their ideas and actions) operate?
(ii) what can be done to lessen its influence?

My own short-list of the answers to question (i) is:

(a) Social workers especially, but clients too, develop their own implicit theories as to the nature and aetiology of the difficulties before them; for example, that an in-depth discussion has powerful behaviour-changing properties in its own right; or, in the case of clients, that problems of child behaviour have their origins almost exclusively in genetic factors. Sometimes these implicit assumptions are so fundamental as to escape detection altogether. It was not until the clients were independently interviewed in the Mayer and Timms study [6] that they articulated their views: that, for example, the historical/development of attitude of workers to their problems was at odds with their own experience of these difficulties as contemporary and practical.

(b) It is in the nature of the human perceptual apparatus to go well beyond the available evidence [10]. Contrary to how it often seems to the busy social worker, even the most intensively-visited clients live 98% of their lives outside the influence of professional helpers. There is, therefore, often a mass of complicated material to make sense of and relate to one or two key themes. In such circumstances, it is impossible not to jump to some conclusions to try to impose (not always accurately) some pattern on events.

(c) Why do clients not correct these misperceptions when they spot them? Some do, of course, and some social workers listen carefully when this happens. But even to ask this question is to ignore firstly, the tremendous power differences between anxious, verbally-unsophisticated, working class clients and their predominantly middle-class, relatively unanxious, verbally sophisticated helpers and, secondly, the established practices of a profession which is only now beginning to kick its long-established habit of regarding the testimony of clients as so much raw material thinly salted through with clues as to 'underlying pathology'. This pathology was once viewed through individual, stage-developmental, fixation-related propositions [11] [12]; today, there is a good chance that it will be viewed in terms of patterns of disordered family functioning [13] [14] or through a set of socio-political assumptions [15]. With one or two important differences [16] [17] the same could be said of the increasingly influential behavioural approaches.

This discussion is not a plea for less explicit theorising or less interpretation. Implicit theorising is far more dangerous because it is rarely available for public scrutiny and criticism. The point is that we cannot not interpret the evidence of our senses, but we could try harder to control our use of theory and interpretation so that the client has a chance to share in and to influence this process.

(d) Finally there are 'demand effects', the unaccountable tendency of subjects without very strong feelings (and sometimes with) to give their questioners the information they think they would like to hear. As psychologists, psychotherapy researchers [18] [19] and market researchers know to their cost, great care and considerable artifice is required to extract uncoloured information from respondents.

In answer to question (ii) the arguments so far suggest that social work's acceptance of subjectivity, unbridled eclecticism, exclusively verbal and qualitative assessment and evaluation, and 'open-plan' (unstructured, blank-sheet) case recording, is very questionable. If we are to begin to square up to some of the distorting influences ranged against us, we must develop a more critical approach to questions of evidence, and a more robust set of evaluation practices.

Fortunately, much of the groudwork has already been done. In Single Case Experimental Designs and the assessment approaches that go with them, there is on offer an evaluation technology which is both rigorous, flexible, and well-attuned to the relatively small-scale individual and family problems which remain the main focus of social work.

ORIGINS AND HISTORY OF SINGLE CASE EXPERIMENTATION

The application of Single Case Experimental Designs to clinical work stems from the work of a British psychologist [20] [21] [22] who used prototype A B A design (pre-intervention fixing of the rate of a piece of problematic behaviour – followed by intervention – followed by a withdrawal of intervention) in a range of cases including one involving paranoid delusions [23]. Shapiro's achievement was to bring together the traditional concern in psychology and psychiatry for the unique individual and his problems, and the idea of careful experimentation to determine outcome, which was at this time the exclusive province of group-comparison research.

The next phase of rapid development took place as a result of the work of Chassan [24] and the explosive growth of the various clinical approaches based upon operant learning theory [25] known collectively as Behaviour Modification. Key features of this approach are the systematic introduction and removal of therapeutic or situational factors while the monitoring of behaviour continues in respect of a number of key variables.

Such measurement techniques are now in widespread use not only in clinic-based programmes, but also in field settings [17] [26]. The social work literature has thrown up spasmodic contributions on this theme, in general suggesting that these approaches show considerable promise for at least part of our work, describing the main methods, and giving one or two examples.

However, these examples present some problems. Firstly the numbers of actual instances of their use is low. Secondly, the approach is made to seem rather 'pat' in some, as if there were no inherent difficulties apart from the question of the knowledge and skill of the practioner. Thirdly, there is a tendency to choose problems which seem rather nicely discrete, or well-circumscribed. However, this is not true of all the contributions [27] [28] [29] [30] [31] [32] [33] [34].

For me these methods are the most important contribution of Behaviour Modification approaches to social work. Moreover, as the reader will see, they do not actually require adherence to any particular therapeutic approach.

My experience of using and teaching single case evaluation designs (S.C.E.Ds) [17] [35] convinces me that the main difficulties of the approach lie not in persuading clients to co-operate, not in the production of graphs, but in the early stages of choosing and defining the parameters to be measured. The social work literature on S.C.E.Ds is not as helpful as it might be here. Successful use of S.C.E.Ds depends upon a number of prior assessment stages. These are as follows:

(i) Negotiations have to take place about what the various definitions which surround referrals mean in terms of actual behaviour or specific influence. We need to know what an 'inadequate personality' [36] or a 'paranoid reaction' means in respect of who does what, where, how often, and with what apparent consequences? One cannot measure 'an inferiority complex'; we have to decide what someone who is supposed to have one of these does too much, or too little of, to so earn themselves the title. All this is necessary for technical reasons but it has other consequences, as when a careful analysis of 'disturbed behaviour' on the part of a schoolchild, maps out as: interfering with the work of other pupils, making unexpected noises, leaving his desk without permission, and occasionally hitting classmates without apparent provocation [17]. The problem is still serious, but the negative impact of the psychopathological 'labelling' of the earlier definition is reduced.

(ii) Two or three key elements or reliable indicators of the problem(s) have to be selected: clearly distinguishable behaviours, or patterns of interaction which, though not sufficient to encompass the whole, are nevertheless necessary conditions of it, and co-vary reliably with the presence and magnitude of it. This is not as easy in field or residential work as it can be elsewhere in the helping professions. Social work problems tend to be broad in scope and ill-defined, or, conversely, over-defined by other would-be helpers prior to referral. They may also be well-immunised against change by previous abortive attempts at solution; made up of many different interacting elements, and are sometimes problems of relationships between people, not just the problems *of* people. So the difficulties of this stage should not be underestimated. Nevertheless, it is possible in some cases to decide that, for example, references to surveillance, or messages coming through the TV, are the essence of 'paranoid reaction', failure to initiate conversations and to maintain short periods of eye contact are at the centre of Mr X's 'social inadequacy', and Mr Y's outbursts of temper are related to Mrs Y's anxious withdrawal, and vice versa. Readers must judge for themselves the validity of such indicators, but should bear in mind that such exercises are always to some extent arbitrary – they are educated guesses which are tested out later.

(iii) This process of convergence and specification requires practice simply because it runs counter to many of the established methods of the profession. Students tend to receive praise for the complexity of their case-formulations. Yet what is required here is not a long series of flexible, multi-purpose goals, but a few inflexible, and discrete-as-possible goals, based upon hypotheses about what is wrong in the situation and how it might be put right. These ideas are consistent with certain practices in the natural sciences, where the hallmark of good practice is the construction of tests which could easily fail; which in Popper's terms [27] are as 'risky' as possible. Only in this way do we obtain clear feedback on our case-experiments. Protean goals and indicators, capable of endless re-interpretation and re-appraisal in the light of threatening evidence, though easier to live with in the short term, are ultimately self-defeating. In using them we rob ourselves of clear feedback on progress, and therefore of an opportunity to substitute new and more relevant objectives for old. Dealing in behaviour, or clearly distinguishable events, substantially reduces the risk of the 'Kafkaesque' effect referred to earlier in the context of consumer-opinion research.

(iv) Single Case Designs introduce a quantitative element into case evaluation. This is not to say that qualitative variables, such as how people feel about their situation, should or can be ignored. An increased level of contact between natural parents and foster child may look nice on a graph, but if all concerned continue to dislike it, then is this the most relevant assessment point? The sensible approach is to use quantitative alongside qualitative assessment so that each reinforces the other. Thus, reports of a 'better atmosphere' in the hostel may need closer investigation (they may be due to demand-effects) if the amount of time residents spend in communal activities is in sharp decline. Alternatively, the problem could be reassessed in terms of a need for more personal space or for freedom from communal pressures. The main characteristic of qualitative assessment based on experimental principles is that end-states, which are as closely defined as possible, should be pre-decided. This can be done by asking clients and other interested parties to typify the present features of their problems, and then to typify what would be happening if there were a substantial improvement. In my experience, clients do this readily: 'We'd talk to each other, and consult each other more, and wouldn't be so afraid to say how we felt about things for fear of bringing on a row or a sulking session ...'.

This last statement contains four potentially quantifiable elements.

(v) Having selected representative indicators, the next step is to produce a sample of the relevant pre-intervention behaviour, that is, pre-specific, problem-countering, pre-assessment intervention: sometimes just assessing a problem alters it – normally for the better. This is known as a baseline, or base-rate measure, and is the standard against which progress is measured. The aim here is to produce a representative sequence, that is a typical range or pattern, continuing long enough for odd fluctuations to iron out or be seen in context. Therefore, length of recording will vary according to the frequency of the behaviour. Periods of rumination in a case of clinical depression, or obsessive-cumpulsive rituals from a severely neurotic client, being high-frequency, will yield representative samples in a short time. Enuresis and stealing will usually be low in frequency and will need a much longer period of observation. Having some yardstick against which to measure improvement is an advance on traditional methods where often there is only a hazy impression of the status quo ante.

(vi) Space here is too limited to allow a full discussion of recording methods [27] [38]. In essence, success in persuading clients or mediators to co-operate depends on clear, matter-of-fact explanations about the purpose and the advantages of so doing, clear and well-produced proforma (clients need not be troubled with graphs; diaries are better and can be used to record both occurrences and reflections), rehearsal of any likely difficulties, and the social worker actually using the results in front of the clients. Observation and recording can be carried out by a wide range of people in different parts of the client's environment, or by clients themselves. If no basis for co-operation emerges, then this approach to evaluation cannot proceed, but then therapeutic gains would be likely to be minimal anyway.

DIFFERENT TYPES OF S.C.E.D.

A.B. Methods

The simplest design is the A.B. 'before and after' comparison (see Fig. 1). This is the one most often used in social work settings and can give much useful correlational information. It is, however, quasi-experimental only, as will become clear later.

This example is an extract from a three month project to maintain a disruptive (or as the head teacher preferred 'disturbed') schoolboy in the normal school provision rather than a specialised unit. The scheme has much in common with modern delinquency-prevention and de-labelling schemes.

The main methods used were:

(i) encouraging teachers to respond to reasonable behaviour and ignore most of the bad (the opposite contingencies applied previously);

Fig 1. Data from a classroom management scheme for a 'disturbed' nine year old boy.

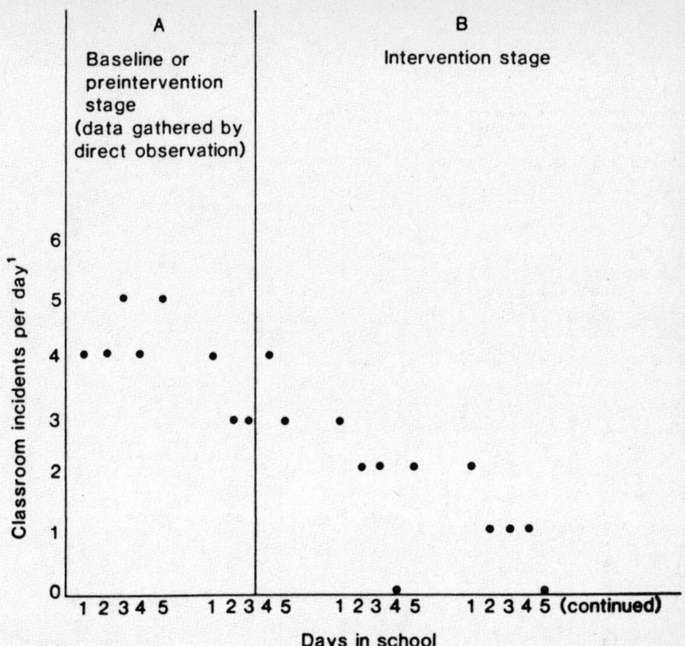

[1]Predefined with teachers as any combination of: Interfacing with the work of others; causing physical pain to others; leaving his seat and failing to return within one minute of first being asked; making loud noises, or noises continuing long enough to distract other pupils.

(Source: Sheldon [17])

(ii) a time-out scheme for episodes of violence to replace heavy 'psychological' sessions with well-intentioned staff – who were (unwittingly) positively reinforcing this bad behaviour;
(iii) a points scheme linking home and school [17].

On follow-up at fourteen weeks and six months the disruptive behaviour was well under control and the child continued to be taught at his ordinary school.

Fig. 2 presents a piece of work by a probation student to check out his withdrawn client's responsiveness to social skills training. The gains are modest but worthwhile, and gave a considerable boost of confidence to a client who tended to see his inhibited behaviour as unalterable. Note the incorporation of a follow-up period. There are one or two problems with the graph, not least the rising and rather

Fig 2. AB Design with follow up: Social Skill Training with a Withdrawn Client.

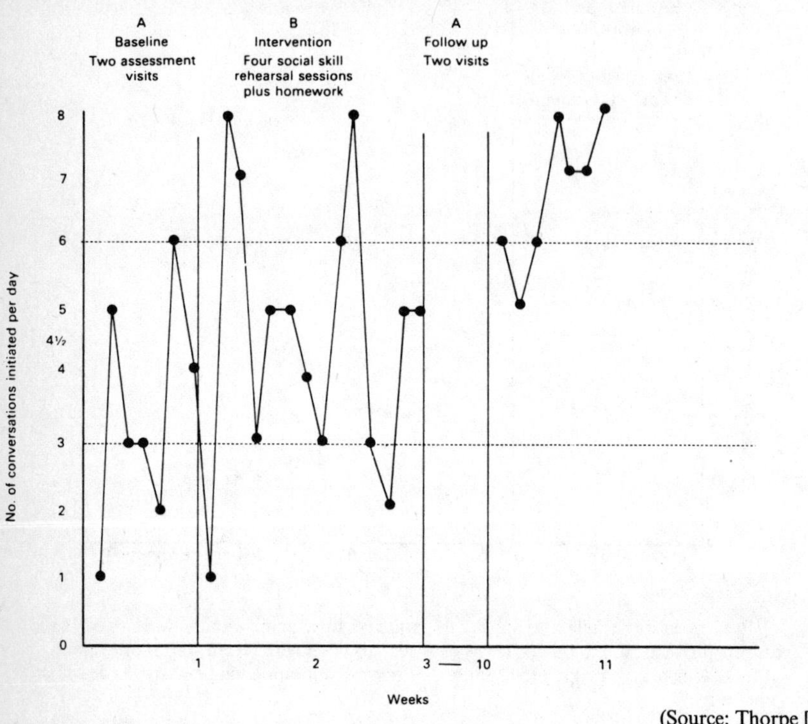

(Source: Thorpe [39])

unstable baseline, but field studies are seldom as tidy as one might wish. Ideally, the student should have continued to monitor for a longer period to see if the marked fluctuations would moderate, but then clients who stoically cope with problems for years often get suddenly impatient when help seems at hand.

I have given considerable space to the least sophisticated designs for the simple reason that these correlational studies are likely to have most relevance to routine social work for some time to come. However, they do present problems as Fig. 3 illustrates.

The hypothetical relationship in Fig. 3 demonstrates that in A.B. designs the social worker may be intervening at a fortuitous moment in the natural course of a problem. We have known for many years that certain problems and conditions

Fig 3. Hypothetical natural course of problems encountered on discharge from psychiatric hospital.

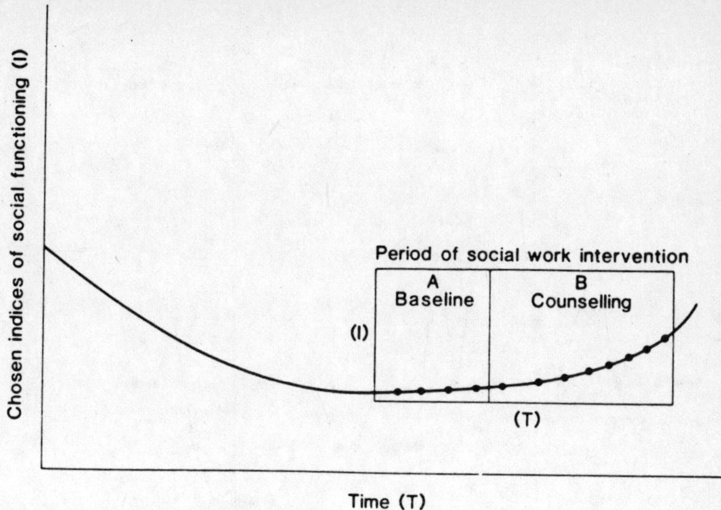

(Source: Sheldon [17])

'spontaneously remit' [40] [41] and although the misattribution of good news may not worry the busy social worker much, there remains the question of replication and a set of wider disciplinary concerns to do with the improvement of our methods.

In order to check whether a particular approach is responsible for a given effect, further phases have to be added.

A.B.A. Designs

The inclusion of a return-to-baseline phase gives two points of comparison:- between A[1] and B and B and A[2] and considerable levels of coincidence are necessary if a behaviour first alters one way as the intervention scheme is applied, then another, as the scheme is suspended or reversed. In some cases, where rapid learning effects are expected, the second A phase can be used as a check on progress and if rates remain favourable, then the scheme can be terminated pending later follow-up. In Fig. 4, as in most cases of its type, the aim is to see whether the controlling variables (in this case, the incidence of parental attention and over-harsh

Fig 4. ABA Design: Behaviour Problems in a 7 year old Mentally Retarded Child at Home.

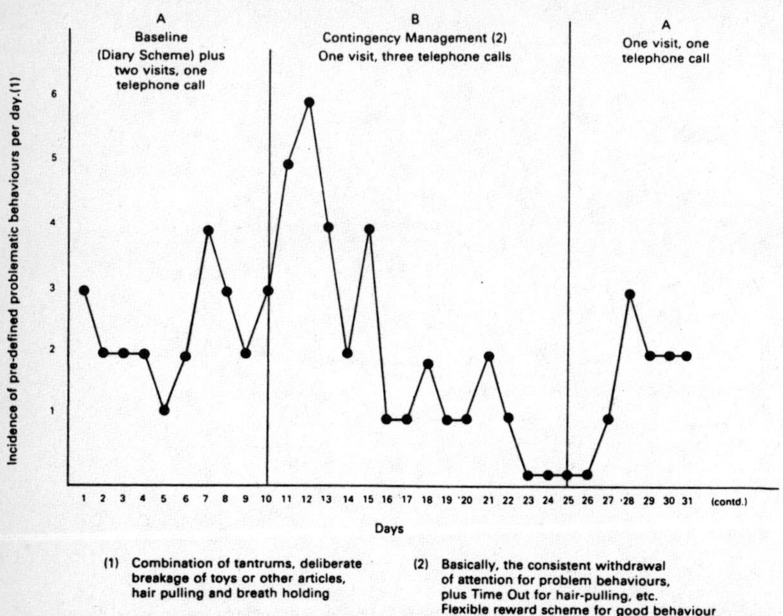

disciplinary practices) are as hypothesised. The fact that, following the typical period of testing-out, the problematic behaviours fall in the B phase (parents could not remember a day free of it in the previous six months), and then increase as the scheme is halted, is strong evidence in favour of this proposition. In this case a further B phase (contingency management) was instituted, to very good effect.

B.A.B. Intervention First Designs

In certain cases it is inadvisable to wait before attempting to make changes and it is perfectly possible to intervene and monitor at the same time; suspend the scheme once it appears to be producing clear effects, and then restart it again. Such designs suit operant behavioural techniques or forms of environmental manipulation. In Fig. 5 the 'urgency' in the case stems from the fact that the child subject was beginning to attract quasi-psychiatric descriptions such as 'withdrawn'. In fact he was a shy, rather under-socialised West Indian boy in a predominantly white nursery school. With the co-operation of two junior members of staff his behaviour was gently shaped away from tearful isolation towards co-operative play.

Fig 5. Withdrawn behaviour in a four year old nursery school child.

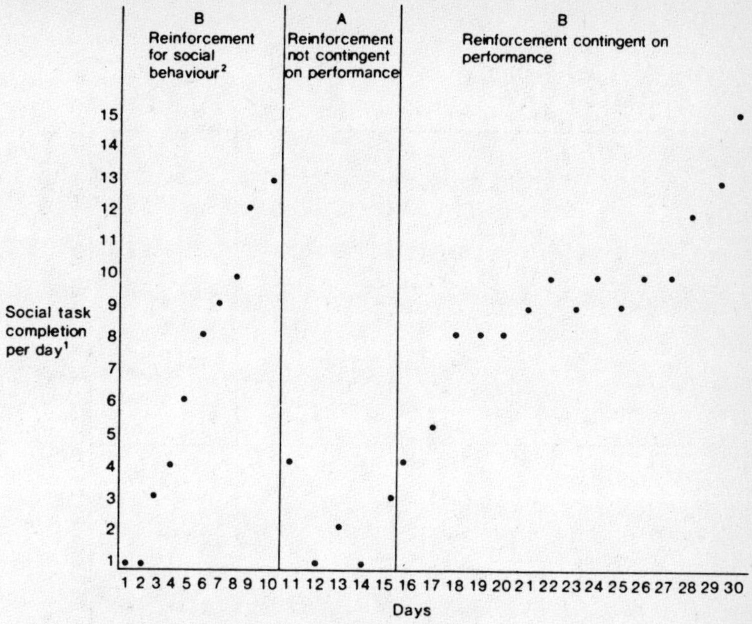

[1] Predefined tasks (behaviour shaping, ranging from showing interest in play of others, to solitary play nearby, to participatory play).
[2] Approval plus sweets (given by nursery staff).

(Source: Sheldon [17])

A.B.A.B. Designs

The most satisfactory design from a case-research point of view poses the greatest practical and ethical difficulties. In this approach a 'therapeutic' influence is first compared to a baseline measure of key indicators, withdrawn or deliberately reversed, and then reintroduced. Fig. 6 is an example featuring an attempt to reduce the overstimulation at the hands of her parents of a young woman suffering from schizophrenia. Their habit was to enquire into, discuss and attempt to refute her delusional preoccupations regarding electronic and other forms of surveillance. The family were advised to ignore delusional references, but to respond encouragingly to other patterns of conversation. This study is simply one part of the attempt to help this client and is concerned with the management of a problem which family members found very difficult to cope with and which, it was hypothesised, was tied up with periodic requests for her removal to hospital.

Fig 6. Contingency management scheme for reducing delusional talk in twenty four year old psychiatric out-patient.

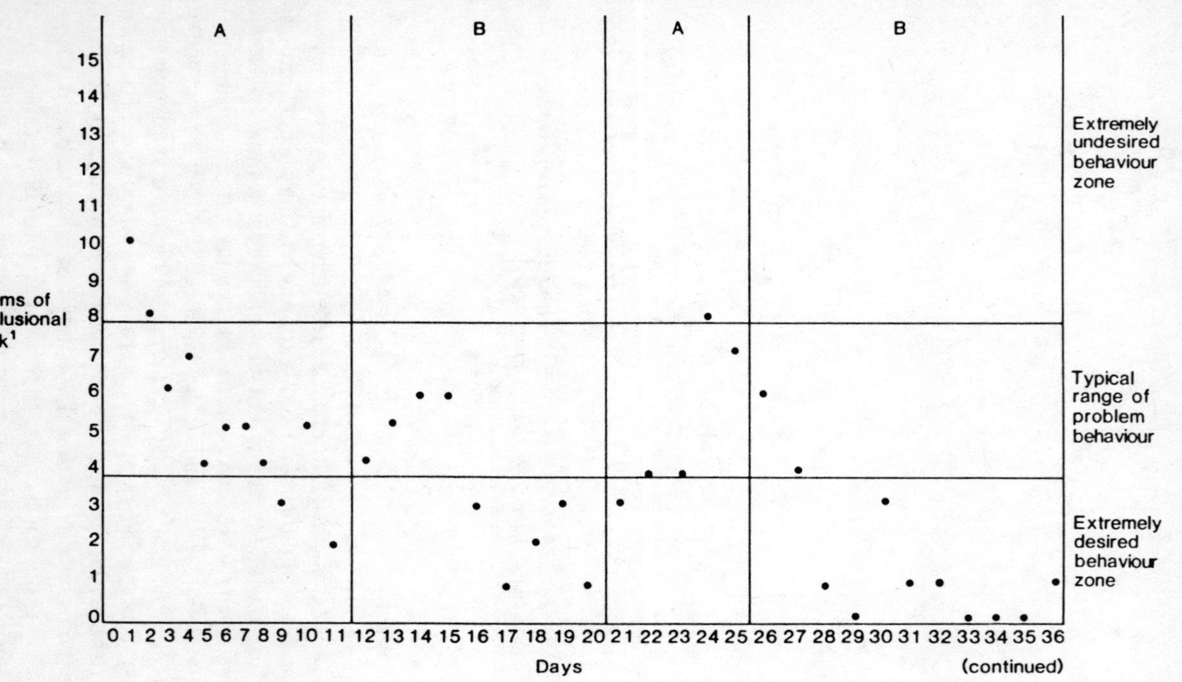

[1] Operationally defined with relatives.

(Source: Sheldon [17])

Fig 7. Multiple baseline design: Disciplining problems in a single parent family.

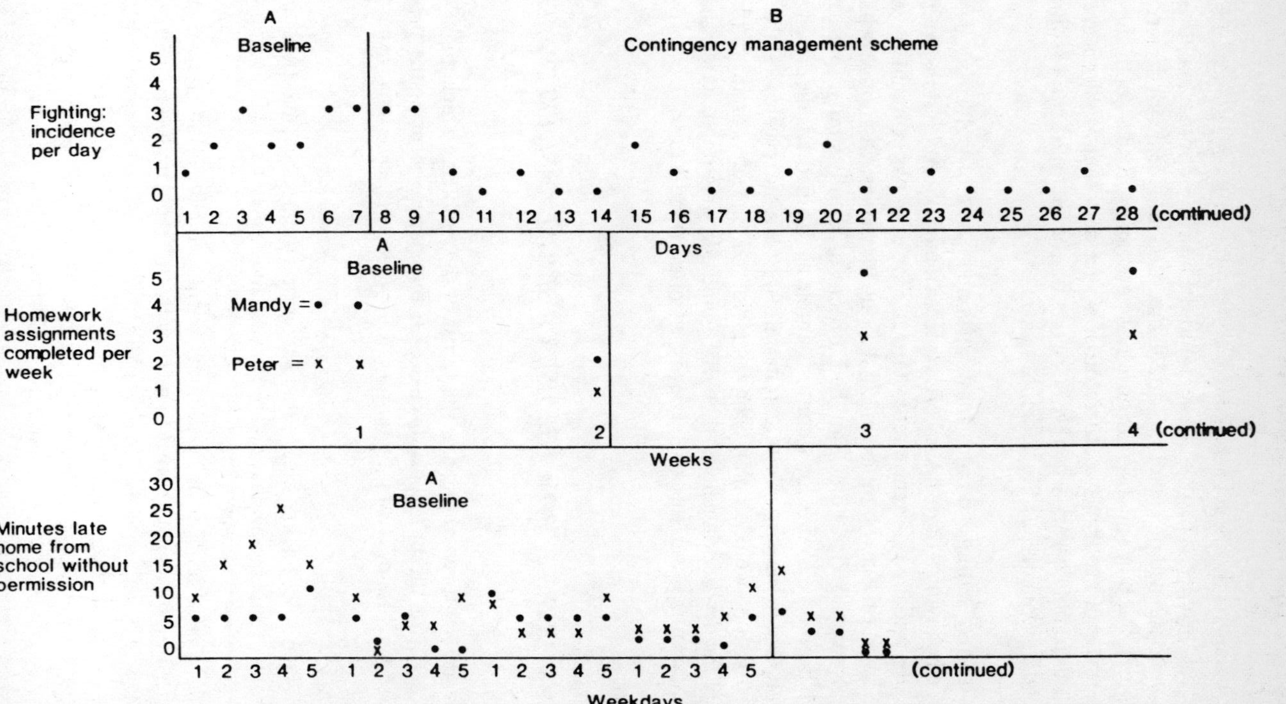

[1] Programme equals: reinforcement of cooperative behaviour with star chart, sweets, models, comics, plus extra TV time and bonus outings with social worker, determined on a sliding scale. Also agreed rates for deprivation of privileges.

(Source: Sheldon [17])

Multiple Baselines and Baselines Across Settings Designs

Social problems rarely come in tidy single units. Often it is necessary to deal with a number of problems at once. The multiple baseline approach allows this. Problems are baselined one at a time, and the method and incidence decided upon is then applied. The point of observation here is between the B phase of problem one and the A phase of problem two, therefore it is necessary that problems are fairly discrete, and do not co-vary when work begins on the first of them. Methods are thus applied in sequence, as Fig. 7 demonstrates.

'Baselines across settings' designs may be applied where a given sequence of problematic behaviour, or problems arising from a lack of certain skills, occur in a range of substantially different circumstances. For example, it might have been possible to handle the case outlined in Fig. 1 along these lines. Disruptive behaviour of a kind also occurred at home and, had it been sufficiently similar in character, could have been used to provide a control sample as the methods described above were first applied to the school setting. If monitoring at home revealed a stable base-rate of disruption, while similar behaviours in school were coming under the influence of the new contingencies, then this would add weight to the view that any behavioural changes were due to the newly introduced influences.

PROBLEMS ARISING FROM THE USE OF SINGLE CASE EXPERIMENTAL DESIGNS

I have already put forward the view that most of the problems which might defeat the application of the principles discussed in this paper, occur at the problem-definition stage. Aside from these, the following obstacles may need to be overcome:

1. It is only sensible to acknowledge that sometimes therapeutic objectives, and the goals of careful outcome-evaluation are at odds, and that some kind of compromise between rigour and relevance must be attempted. Studies exist which show that when student psychologists are evaluating clients on clinical outcome-measures they tend to hunt for snake phobics to work with and avoid multi-problem families like the plague. Needless to say, this would be particularly senseless in the case of social work. The methods must serve our interests, and not the reverse. Often this problem can be handled by using S.C.E.Ds to evaluate one part of a programme and rigorous qualitative procedures to supplement these. There exists now a continuum of evaluation procedures and we should respond accordingly [34].

2. Suspending and reversing therapeutic inputs causes some problems for social workers and I can think of cases of my own where I might have pursued these rather too enthusiastically. However, there is a powerful demonstration-effect to be had, for example when parents see that their behaviour and that of the children is closely related.

3. Strictly speaking, the changes that occur and do not occur in S.C.E.Ds can tell us nothing for sure about how to handle other cases that appear to be similar. This is the issue of representativeness, or external validity. In practice human beings do tend to generalise from specific situations to a range of apparently similar circumstances, but our feelings about the applicability of certain of the methods we have tested in two or three cases must be put to the test in each successive encounter.

CONCLUSIONS

Social workers have the opportunity with these methods to have the best of both worlds – to test out the theoretical propositions they obtain from others, and to follow through on their own hunches about what might work; to use rigorous evaluation devices, and yet take full account of individual differences and idiosyncracies in their application. These experimental and quasi-experimental approaches can be used in conjunction with other, more familiar (but sadly, rarely spelled-out) qualitative methods – and in fact are better for being used in combination. Moreover, there is nothing to suggest that these approaches need be applied in an excessively 'mechanical' way, or that they are the sole preserve of behaviourists. The position is simply that few other kinds of therapists make use of them. To the extent that this is because they cannot accommodate tangible, pre-set indicators of outcome into their methods (the only pre-requisite) our suspicions should be aroused.

References

1. Powers, E. & Witmer, H. An Experiment in the Prevention of Delinquency – the Cambridge Somerville Youth Study. Columbia University Press, New York, 1951.

2. Meyer, H., Borgatta, E. & Jones, W. Girls at Vocational High. Russell Sage Foundation, New York, 1965.

3. Bergin, A.E. 'The Evaluation of Therapeutic Outcomes' in Bergin, A.E. & Garfield S.L. (Eds.) Handbook of Psychotherapy and Behaviour Change. Wiley, New York, 1971.

4. Rachman, S.J. & Wilson, G.T. The Effects of Psychological Therapy. Oxford University Press, 1980 (2nd edition).

5. Fischer, J. The Effectiveness of Social Casework. Charles C. Thomas, Springfield, Illinois, 1976.
6. Mayer, J.E. & Timms, N. The Client Speaks. Routledge & Kegan Paul, London, 1970.
7. Rees, S.J. 'No More than Contact: An Outcome of Social Work' British Journal of Social Work. 4, 3, 1974, 255-79.
8. Rees, S.J. & Wallace, A. Verdicts on Social Work. Edward Arnold, London, 1982.
9. Maluccio, A.N. Learning from Clients. Free Press, London, 1979.
10. Gregory, R. Eye and Brain. Weidenfeld & Nicolson, London, 1979.
11. Erikson, E. Childhood and Society. Pelican, 1967.
12. Hollis, F. Casework: A Psychosocial Therapy. Random House, New York, 1968.
13. Satir, V. Conjoint Family Therapy. Science and Behaviour Books, New York, 1964.
14. Selvini-Palazzoli, M., Bascolo, L., Cechin, G & Prata, G. Paradox and Counter Paradox. Aronson, New York, 1978.
15. Corrigan, P. & Leonard, P. Social Work Practice under Capitalism. Macmillan, London, 1978.
16. Sheldon, B. 'Theory and Practice in Social Work: A Re-examination of a Tenuous Relationship' British Journal of Social Work. 8, 11, 1978.
17. Sheldon B. Behaviour Modification: Theory, Practice and Philosophy. Tavistock, London, 1982.
18. Heine, R. 'A Comparison of Patients' Reports on Psychotherapeutic Experience with Psychoanalytic, Non-Directive and Adlerian Therapists' American Journal of Psychotherapy. 7, 1953.
19. Bandura, A. Principles of Behaviour Modification. Holt Rinehart, New York, 1969.
20. Shapiro, M.B. & Ravenette, A.T. 'A Preliminary Experiment on Paranoid Delusions' Journal of Mental Science. 105, 1959, 295-312.
21. Shapiro, M.B. 'The Single Case in Clinical-Psychological Research' Journal of General Psychology. 74, 1966, 3-23.
22. Shapiro, M. 'The Single Case in Fundamental Clinical Psychological Research' British Journal of Medical Psychology. 34.1961, 255-263.
23. Hersen, M. & Barlow, D.H. Single Case Experimental Designs. Pergamon, Oxford, 1976.
24. Chassan, J.B. Research Design in Clinical Psychology and Psychiatry. Appleton Crafts, New York, 1967.
25. Skinner, B.F. Science and Human Behaviour. Collier-Macmillan, London, 1953.
26. Oliver, J. 'The Behavioural Treatment of a Case of Obsessional House Cleaning in a Personality Disordered Client' International Journal of Behavioural Social Work. 1, 1, 1981, 39-54.
27. Bloom, M. The Paradox of Helping. Wiley, New York, 1975.
28. Fischer, J. & Gochros, H. Planned Behaviour Change. Free Press, New York, 1976.
29. Green, J.K. & Morrow, W.R. 'Precision Social Work : General Model and Illustrative Student Projects with Clients' Education for Social Work. 1972, 19-29.
30. Howe, M.W. 'Using Clients' Observations in Research' Social Work. 21, 1, 1976.
31. Man Keung Ho 'Evaluation as a Means of Treatment' Social Work. 21, 1, 1976, 24-27.
32. Jayaratne, S. 'Single Subject and Group Designs in Treatment Evaluation' Social Work Research & Abstracts. 1977, 35-42.
33. Bloom, M. & Block, S.R. 'Evaluating One's Own Effectiveness and Efficiency' Social Work. 22, 1977, 130-136.

34. Gambrill, E. & Barth, R. 'Single Case Study Desings Revisited' Social Work Research and Abstracts. 16, 3, 1980, 15-20.

35. Sheldon, B. 'The Use of Single Case Experimental Designs in the Evaluation of Social Work' British Journal of Social Work. 13, 1983, 477-500.

36. Hudson, B. 'An Inadequate Personality' Social Work Today. 6, 16, 1975.

37. Popper, K. Conjectures and Refutations. Routledge & Kegan Paul, London, 1963.

38. Sheldon, B. Evaluation-Oriented Case Recording. Scottish Office, 1984.

39. Thorpe, N. Unpublished Student Report. University of Birmingham, 1983.

40. Eysenck, H.J. 'The Effects of Psychotherapy: An Evaluation' Journal of Consulting Psychology. 16, 1952, 319-24.

41. Eysenck, H.J. The Effects of Psychotherapy, Handbook of Abnormal Psychology. Pitman Medical, London, 1960.

The Priority of Client Evaluations

Alison Wallace and Stuart Rees

In evaluations of social work and other personal social services, we have argued elsewhere [1] that clients' judgements are the most important criteria. Our insistence on the highest priority being attached to clients' evaluations derives in part from our belief that social workers' accountability to clients takes precedence over accountability to agency or profession.

It is not just a matter of cynicism to argue that the jobs of social workers and the survival of agencies depend on the existence of large numbers of people who are dependent, financially and in other ways. Our views about the primacy of clients' evaluations in any enquiry into the effects and effectiveness of social work are based not only on ideological but also professional and practical considerations. We will try first to unmask our ideological stance by looking at certain political and professional concerns.

(A) POLITICAL

At the baseline of our belief in the value of consumer evaluation is a particular view of the function of social work. Social work's major task is to respond to problems which have largely been thrown up by an economic and cultural system which operates for the considerable benefit of some and results in the exploitation and suffering of others. In response to these problems, social workers' responsibility is never to lose sight of the needs of the most powerless people and to work not only to meet those needs but also to raise aspirations where they appear to have been too fatalistic, too conservative. These goals are related to our convictions about the relevance to social work of socialist principles concerned with a more equal and more just society. In the pursuit of such objectives, social workers' priorities would be focused not just on policies concerned with the distribution of resources but also on the quality of human relationships in a variety of contexts. Such goals would not be achieved by social workers acting alone but would require them to make alliances with those who shared the same concerns, including client groups and, of course, colleagues in social welfare, whatever their status or professional standing.

Our belief in the value of client evaluation derives from the ideologically based point of view just expressed. Evaluative criteria should focus on accountability to clients' interests, and most important, to those people least able to help themselves. We deliberately link such accountability to questions of appropriateness: the most telling means of assessing accountability is in terms of the appropriateness of social work to the interests of the most powerless citizens. Such a statement implies the desirability of explicit, ideologically based commitments which enable social workers, researchers and policy makers to say what their priorities are and on what grounds they have chosen them. We do not think that such a belief hinders the conduct of evaluative research. On the contrary, the pretence that values do not influence the choice of research interests and methods is more likely to produce bias than the explicitness that we have just documented. As Becker [2] has stated, in social research 'we can never avoid taking sides ... our problem is to make sure that whatever point of view we take, our research meets the standards of good scientific work'.

(B) PROFESSIONAL

We would also argue that the client is the ultimate expert on what kind of service is supportive and useful. It is thus crucial in any evaluation exercise that clients are given the chance to speak for themselves, and to provide their own judgement of the services that are, and are not provided. Our experience is that given the opportunity, time and adequate and sensitive research techniques, clients have very well-developed critical faculties which they can use to enlighten organisations in three crucial areas,

1. their own assessments of their needs;
2. their assessments of an organisation's performance or ability to meet these needs;
3. their assessments of the appropriateness of an agency's objectives.

Clients' needs, as assessed by clients themselves, must be the starting point of such service providers. Indeed, the ethical and political justification for the existence of such services is that ordinary people allegedly benefit from them and would benefit even more if the employed professionals could demonstrate the kind of competence which is valued highly by consumers [3]. However, research provides numerous illustrations of clients judging professional practice as incompetent. Such incompetence is related, among other things, to the development of misunderstandings based on differing expectations, values and orientations to problem-solving between social workers and clients [4]. If service providers, be they lawyers, teachers, doctors, social workers, want to improve on their current practices, they should take seriously clients' views. There are also considerable advantages in eliciting clients' views. There are also considerable advantages in eliciting clients' assessments of the appropriateness of an agency's objectives. There are dangers in evaluating an agency in terms of its self-defined goals: clients may not recognise the legitimacy of such objectives [5].

At this point, some of the wider political and economic events which have influenced the uses of client evaluations need to be considered. After that discussion we will examine the methodological obstacles in conducting client studies and in combining client views with other criteria.

CONTROVERSIES OVER CLIENT EVALUATION

The influence of political consideratons on the uses of client evaluations is apparent in historical developments of the past 20 years. In the 60's and early 70's the War on Poverty programmes in America underlined the importance of 'people power', the ideal that consumer and client opinion mattered. The political commitment that followed from this ideal saw the emergence of numerous community groups, tenants' association and citizens' rights bureaus throughout the United States. This was soon followed in Britain by the Urban Community Development Projects and a little later in Australia by the attempt to decentralise government and professional control through the Australian Assistance Plan.

Parallel to the insistence on community development as a solution to social problems was the increasing consumer challenge to professional interests not merely in activities such as social work. Ordinary people's dismay with the legal profession's control over even simple matters such as the purchase of a house encouraged people to do their own conveyancing. Publicity associated with China's bare-foot doctors and other forms of alternative medicine has produced challenges to the dominance of doctors in controlling people's health care. In Australia the development of Aboriginal legal and medical services bears witness to a small minority group's disenchantment with conventional, professional ways of running services.

Various writers and researchers encouraged these developments. In 1970 Mayer and Timms carried out client evaluations of social work services because they thought that client opinion had previously been 'neglected' [6]. Others argued that consumer views confirmed the judgements of professionals and for that reason such client opinion should always be sought in evaluations of services [7]. Some writers argued that it was 'insolent' if professionals proposed reforms but ignored the views of clients because, traditionally, such views had not been used to influence welfare policies [8].

In spite of the 60's and 70's fascination with client opinion, it would be false to presume that the professions generally have accepted the value of client evaluation. In social work and social administration circles, the resistance to collecting and using client evaluation is still evident, from senior policy and executive level down to front line staff. At management level, the most extreme view we have encountered advocates the rejection of client evaluation on the grounds that it is the fashionable concern of a few political trendies. However, a more typical response is that client evaluation is based on good intentions but is devoid of any practical consequences [1]. Academic critics, on the other hand, have been concerned about the difficulties of conducting consumer evaluation studies and have been sceptical about what could be inferred from the findings [9]. Others have been determined to use clinical trials to demonstrate social worker's 'ineffectiveness' and in so doing ignore some contrary opinion from client evaluation studies [10] [11], though in recent experiments there are signs of a match between client views and those of outside observers [30].

In the questions which critics pose about the usefulness of client evaluation, three themes can be identified.

1. The alleged difference between 'perception' and 'evaluation': a typical question is, 'eliciting clients' responses to services is all very well, but have clients actually evaluated rather than merely perceived?'

2. A second theme concerns the appropriateness of clients' evaluations. A common response from practitioner, researchers and policy makers is that consumer evaluation is appropriate only in certain circumstances. For example, consumer evaluation is appropriate with some clients, but not with others, in some evaluative tasks, but not others.

3. Perhaps the most common objection to client evaluations concerns their reliability. Practitioners and academics dispute the weight that can be attached to clients' views.

These three themes and the doubts contained in them will be discussed.

1. PERCEPTION AND EVALUATION

The claim that clients' judgements represent perception not evaluation is based on a false premise, that the one can be separated from the other. We find this 'perception-not-evaluation-argument' puzzling. The implication is that others' evaluations, be they social workers', or researchers', are somehow different from clients', i.e. the professional judgements are not a matter of perception.

Controversy over the distinction between perception and evaluation derives from the old debate regarding 'objectivity' and 'subjectivity' in social science research. We think it is important to conduct this debate by sifting different kinds of data rather than being trapped into thinking that in some kinds of research such as evaluation data will be of two kinds, one of which is far more reliable than the other. In documenting client's opinions [12] [13] and in examining the conclusions derived from client studies [1], it is apparent that most evaluations emerge from perceptions about the value of certain acts. In this respect, Galtung [14] has linked judgements to values yet in his retrospective analysis he has distinguished between them.

'Evaluation is an act ... and consists in the allocation of objects or stimuli of any kind to an element corresponding to 'good', 'neutral', 'bad'. To evaluate is to sort and order stimuli. A value, however, is the principle according to which this sorting or ordering is done.'

The implication of Galtung's definition is that the researcher's task is to unravel what constitutes someone's perception. Value judgements emerge in perceptions for example as opinions about the competence of some person or the appropriateness of some policy. Individuals' judgements about the merits of a practitioner, a service or a policy can be explicitly stated so that they can be openly discussed, monitored, changed over time, recognised as a possible source of conflict and identified as a major influence in programme evaluation. Such explicit documentation and analysis of individuals' judgements enables a researcher to treat such material as a form of evaluation and subsequently to decide what weight to attach to it. This approach avoids both the notion that objective and subjective are easily separable, or that apparent subjective assessments, as in clients' evaluations, can be hidden under the guise of objectivity. Client evaluations are potentially as useful and reliable as those of other observers. In using client evaluations as one means of making judgements about the usefulness of social work and social workers, it is sensible to acknowledge such elements of subjectivity, to make them explicit and to relate them to the contexts in which they occur. In this way researchers can convey not only the meaning of clients' judgements but can also indicate almost simultaneously, the weight which should be attached to them.

THE APPROPRIATENESS OF CLIENT EVALUATION

Many critics claim that some clients' status and predicament makes it almost impossible for them ever to be useful evaluators. Such criticisms occur with regard to those who are viewed as not fully in possession of their faculties and who are powerless in other ways, including clients who are children or who are mentally handicapped. Challenges to clients' views also occur when the individuals concerned, such as those who have multiple problems associated with the effects of long term poverty, are regarded as too steeped in their own problems to evaluate adequately.

This scepticism about clients' evaluations is linked to assumptions about professional expertise, the 'professional as expert' as opposed to 'client as expert'. Evaluation by some clients does indeed threaten some professionals. We would argue that professional evaluation which includes careful attention to clients' views provides for a comparability of judgements which is not possible when clients' views are ignored.

We reject the view that some clients' judgements should not be attributed any worth because in society at large such people are in relatively powerless positions. Every client be they child, prisoner, or mentally handicapped adult, deserves a voice. Some of the most moving and informative accounts of what it was like to be in the care of the social services derived from studies in which children in care were asked about life in institutions [15]. Some of the most important enquiries into the reform of penal institutions have been prompted by the protest of prisoners [16]. Such protests may actually have become riots but at least from the point of view of politicians, such demands to be heard could not be avoided.

This second concern about appropriateness refers to doubts about the inclusion of client views in certain kinds of evaluative research. Typically, studies of effectiveness include judgements about one service being better than another and usually presuppose a certain concern with objective measurement. In consequence, most experimental studies of the effectiveness of social work intervention have not placed much weight on client judgements. Our point would be that it is not always imperative to evaluate personal social services through experimental studies but if such a research design is used, it could and should include clients' views as one assessment criterion. There are good examples, such as Goldberg's 'Helping the Aged' [17] in which client views have been documented and compared with other evaluative measures. Unless experimental trials have included client appraisals there would be no way of knowing whether researchers' assumptions about professionals; objectives and criteria of assessment would have matched the clients'.

Client evaluation is perhaps the most useful means of documenting those aspects of services, needs and appropriateness of services to those needs, which contribute to judgements about a service's effectiveness, cost effectiveness or efficiency.

Although we believe that client evaluation is appropriate for any range of services, from the simplest provision of a practical aid to the provision of multiple-services over a prolonged period of time, we concede that client evaluation is neither simple nor always the same. Methods of client evaluation would have to change according to the nature of the contact being evaluated and to other considerations. Consumers' views about the relationship between their needs and the response of professionals is of primary concern, but this does not preclude a consideration of other matters, including the views of others in the context in which the evaluation is being conducted. Comprehensive evaluation would include the views of service providers and service receivers. For example, it would be essential for the service providers to identify the ingredients of competent performance, to explore personal and institutional requirements in order to design a system that works.

Client opinion is by no means the only yardstick but it is primary and always appropriate. Other criteria will assume added importance if they can be compared to that important baseline, the consumers' views. Those views have been shown to be discriminating, as in distinctions between supportive and unsupportive social workers [31]. They have been linked to the obstacles which affect worker and client co-operation, as in evidence about the resources required to overcome even some aspects of poverty [32].

3. THE RELIABILITY OF CLIENTS' EVALUATIONS

The criticism and doubts about the uses of clients' opinions and evaluations can be overcome by confronting important issues in research methods. These include questions such as which forms of investigation are most appropriate to client evaluations and how to evaluate and identify the meaning of clients' responses.

We now turn to these methodological considerations. As stated earlier, client evaluation although crucial is not an easy research task. A variety of considerations can affect a client's response to service, and a competent researcher must be aware of such considerations and account for them in the methodological approach adopted. Such considerations would include gross variables such as ethnicity, sex, socio-economic status (all of which may be more important to the response than the experience of these individuals as clients); the extent of previous social agency contact (is this the first or fiftieth time that the client has presented?); the extent of contact with other helping agencies, and experience in dealing with those in authority positions; the degree of coercive power the agency has over clients, and the effect of the client worker relationship on evaluations of competence and effectiveness. We now turn to these methodological considerations.

(i) *Desirability Of In-depth Interviews*

A comprehensive evaluation of services by clients is best achieved by in-depth interviews. The priority in client evaluation is to provide the fullest possible understanding of the needs of the client, and of his/her response to the service provided or not provided as the case may be. The rigour of such an approach is not an end in itself but there is no substitute for face to face, semi-structured discussions around a set of topics. A fluid, but client centred approach allows comparable data to be collected from all respondents.

Open-ended questions are an inherent part of in-depth interviewing. Such questioning does lead to problems associated with structuring the interviews and subsequently with problems of coding, processing and analysing, but overcomes the dangers of too tightly controlled interviews as in a list of questions previously determined. The danger of the use of such controlled techniques is the underlying assumption that the important variables are known and understood. This can lead to a distortion of clients' assessments. The questions asked may reflect what the researchers think is relevant – but exclude considerations which are important to the client. Rubenstein and Block [18] made this mistake when exploring clients' opinions about their relationship with the worker. Clients' were not given free rein in their evaluations but instead had to rate workers according to criteria provided by the researchers: the worker's fairness and honesty and the client's feelings of ease with the worker. From the clients' perspective these attributes may not have been the most important aspects of their relationships with the social worker. It is important to recognise that the assumptions that lie behind apparently straightforward questions may not in fact be shared by the client.

Similar criticisms can be made of studies which provide fixed responses to questions, obliging respondents to limit their answers to specified categories, as in ratings of 'satisfactory' or 'unsatisfactory', 'adequate', or 'inadequate'. On their own, such responses are worse than useless. They provide no information as to what it is exactly that clients find satisfactory or unsatisfactory, or for the reasons behind their opinions. In-depth interviewing, on the other hand, can identify issues that make a difference to clients. A skilled interviewer could explore the clients' experience by asking such questions as: what caused the satisfaction/dissatisfaction? What sorts of things made a difference, the service, the personnel, the contrast between this experience and previous ones with other people in positions of authority? Is this the first contact which they have had with a social service agency? At what point in the evaluation process did this occur? What sort of things could be done to improve the situation and make services more useful? Have they received or applied for help from any other agency? Such specific questions and probing interviewing techniques should produce responses which are precise, discriminating and critical. Such linking of clients' evaluations to time, place, people and organisations is not easy. But it is the only way to document specific information on the service response found useful or otherwise by clients in different circumstances, i.e. to evaluate clients;' judgements. Oversimplified questionnaires, the weighting of client satisfaction on a scale or the mere recording of the numbers of 'satisfied' or 'dissatisfied' (unfortunately the research techniques adopted in a depressing number of studies) can never derive such understanding.

Clearly, an adequate research design needs to anticipate the variability in clients responses. Methodology can anticipate and accommodate a high degree of variability by recognising that clients may have little in common, whether in their life styles, or in the more obvious contrasts between statements of satisfaction and dissatisfaction. A good research design would need to account for this variability, and never provide only for simple conclusions and so obliterate rich information about people's differences.

(ii) *Interviewing*

The success of unstructured, in-depth interviewing depends partly on the choice of the interviewer. Ideally, such researchers should be independent from the service-providing agency. Service providers must realise their position of power vis-a-vis the client. Clients may be reluctant to criticise services if contact is current or if they expect future contact with the agency. They may feel that they would be jeopardising their chances of receiving help in the future if they are too critical of service received in the past. For example, research has shown that parents dealing with adoption agencies can feel dissatisfaction and frustration over certain aspects of their contact – yet are reluctant about asking too many questions of the social workers, or openly expressing hostility. As one parent explained '... we did feel so entirely in their (the agency's) hands and nervous about antagonising them in any way – after all, they had the babies!' [19]. It is interesting to observe that this comment was made by a woman who was herself a professional and presumably used to dealing with people in positions of authority. Other clients may consider it inappropriate for them to criticise those who are offering help. Clients' lack of knowledge, combined with lack of confidence and lack of expertise in dealing with 'official' personnel contributes to their view that it is not appropriate for a 'lay person' to evaluate a 'professional'.

For those reasons, researchers should emphasise their distance from the service providers. Researchers should also take great pains to stress that clients' replies will be treated confidentially and that there could be no unpleasant repercussions in relation to any criticism that is made of the service provider. Such precautions may seem obvious yet it is surprising how often those conducting evaluations (particularly in-house evaluations) fail to exhibit such sensitivity. Several projects we reviewed foresaw no methodological problems in the agency being evaluated administering its own questionnaire or completing an interview schedule with a client [20] [21]. Occasionally the particular service providers encountered by the clients have been given the responsibility for the execution of the research [5]. If practising front line social workers are going to conduct evaluation type interviews they must take the precautions which we have listed and be aware of the fact that certain caveats would be placed on their findings.

(iii) *Document Client Evaluations At Several Points In Time*

Clients' expectations and needs vary in relation to the stage in the development of the problem for which they seek help. For example, parents of handicapped children have been shown to have different needs depending on their child's development [22]. Their primary need in the initial stage of discovering that their child is handicapped is for emotional support to help them cope with acute shock and mental stress. Later on, however, their primary need is for practical information and material support. Ideally, research should capture the responses of clients at a variety of stages in the helpseeking contact – before (in ideal circumstances), during and after contact. Such evaluation interviews at different stages of a client's career are time consuming and not always practical. If documenting clients' evaluations before, during and after contact with the service is not possible, then the researchers should attempt to stratify the sample and either include a client population at different stages in the helpseeking process, or confine the study to one stage – being aware that the subsequent findings may be relevant only to that particular context. If retrospective research is all that is possible, care must be taken to recognise that people's needs change over time and a retrospective reconstruction of events may not pick this up. It is frequently difficult for clients to recall aspects of their behaviour which took place even when the aspects of behaviour have to do with attitudes, expectations, and consequent assessments. It is harder to remember beliefs held at a particular point of time than the actions which made up certain events. Sainsbury [23] for example, observed how the retrospective nature of his study made it difficult to interpret clients' expectations at referral, expectations which can have a decisive effect on subsequent evaluations. He found it impossible to be sure whether the apparent realistic initial expectations of many of the families attending the Family Service Unit indicated good work by referral agents or a subsequent tidying up of memories. Clients may also realign their recollections depending on their subsequent experiences; they may overlook matters that troubled them during actual contact if it is some time since they had social work contact [24].

In summary, a major implication of our stress on interviewing consumers at different points in time is that this increases the number of interviews overall and so, because of the constraints of time and cost, will limit the size of the sample. But if researchers want to unravel the meaning of clients' views they will have to sacrifice sample size in favour of richness of content. We believe strongly in this point but acknowledge that there are arguments against it. For example. Shaw [9] argued client studies with small samples have been descriptive and have had no formal hypothesis. He suggests that with small samples minority group opinion may come to exercise a disproportionate opinion amongst consumer groups.

(iv) *Identify What Client Is Evaluating – Person or Service?*

It was clear from our review of client evaluation studies that client's appreciation and positive evaluation of care offered was frequently tied to characteristics of the helping personnel encountered as well as to the actual outcome of their helpseeking experiences. Theoretically, the distinction made in comments pertaining to the social worker, and to the actual service, or to put it another way, the distinction made between 'helper' and 'help' is important. In practice, however, this distinction is often blurred. In making this distinction we are mindful of Reid's famous point that social work researchers have often found that it is impossible to separate the effectiveness of who you are from what you do [25].

Difficulties occur when it is not clear exactly what a client is referring to in his or her appraisal. For example, client respondents seldom make clear distinctions between social worker and social service. Summarising 300 clients' evaluations of their experiences with a Local Authority Social Service Department, McKay, Goldbert, and Fruin [26] commented,

> 'The consumers' feelings of satisfaction were also bound up with their attitudes towards their social workers. Although we tried to differentiate

> between the consumers' attitudes towards the Department, the services received and their individual worker, it proved difficult to achieve.'

It follows that, whenever possible, researchers must be cautious about identifying what it is clients are referring to when they make judgements about services. Given the large part played by the social worker in influencing clients' response to 'social work', it may be that clients would be reluctant to criticize their treatment. As Gohen [27] explained, 'If the service is presented by someone regarded as likeable, well meaning, the clients may feel disloyal and unfair to him if they criticise the service he represents'. Those clients who believe that social workers are doing them a favour rather than providing a service which is their by right may feel similarly.

Alternatively, if clients perceive social workers as being as much victims of 'the system' as themselves – only being able to do so much because of the constraints of a heavy workload, demanding cases and limited resources, their comments are likely to be sympathetic rather than critical. In this connection Robinson [28] observed the appreciative views expressed by the parents of physically/mentally handicapped children about their social workers. He noted,

> 'Even when they (the professionals) are seen as acting in ways that would normally justify criticism there seems to be a common tendency to explain this away in terms of factors like overwork, staff shortages, or lack of resources, rather than to blame the profession personally'.

Factors such as these can account for some research results which even researchers have found puzzling and which have led them to be suspicious of their own study's conclusions. Several have recognised the danger of a 'halo effect' affecting the validity of research conclusions which indicated high satisfaction. This halo effect has been defined as [28] an 'orientation of good will toward the service providers concerned, rather than a reliable picture of people's real life, day-to-day encounters with the services.'

Such observations only reinforce the argument that it is crucial that consumer evaluation studies establish what kind of social worker attributes and/or activities are found helpful or useful by which particular clients, at what stage in the helpseeking process. It may well be as Reid [25] contended and as studies of the attributes of the helpful person in psychotherapy conclude [29] that it is difficult to separate the useful service from the useful person providing the help.

SOME IMPLICATIONS

Our discussion has referred mostly to the attributes in fact to face encounters, but, in social work, probably two thirds of staff time is spent in activities other than face to face contacts. These activities require good administration as in methodical record keeping and skills in negotiations, in particular with other professionals and other key people, including politicians. This other two thirds of activity probably affects the subsequent handling of clients' cases. But, so far, evaluations of social work have not been able to say whether the effective individual as judged by clients, is an equally effective operator, as judged by his peers and superiors, in the other two thirds of his work.

The relationship between effective administration and effective advocacy for specific client groups' common interests may or may not be related directly to those face to face encounters judged by clients to be both helpful and satisfactory. The connection between performance in one sphere of social work and performance in another is the immediate challenge for researchers concerned with evaluation. It represents an exercise in comparing criteria concerned with agency and professional standards with criteria judged relevant by ordinary people. But the simple principle of accountability to the most powerless people, that ideological stance with which we began this essay, demands that such future evaluation must develop clients' views as the baseline for comparison with other criteria. There is no going back to a preoccupation with agency interests for survival, that process which ensured that clients came last!

References

1. Rees, S. & Wallace, A. Verdicts on Social Work. London, Edward Arnold, 1982.
2. Becker, H. 'Whose side are we on?' Social Problems. 14, Winter, 1967.
3. Kimber, S. 'Competence is incompetence, evaluations of a social work student's practice' Contemporary Social Work Education. Vol. 5. No. 2 August, 1982.
4. Rees, A. 'How misunderstanding occurs' in Bailey, R. & Brake, M. Radical Social Work. London, Edward Arnold, 1975.
5. Giordano, P. 'The client's perspective in agency evaluation' Social Work. 22 (1) 1977, 34-9.
6. Mayer, J.E. & Timms, N. The Client Speaks. London, Routledge, 1970.
7. Kisch, A.I. & Reeder, L.J. 'Client evaluation of physician performance' Journal of Health and Social Behaviour. Vol. 10, No. 1, March, 1969.
8. Guttentag, M. 'The insolence of office' The Journal of Social Issues. Vol. 26, No. 3, Summer 1970.
9. Shaw, I. 'Consumer opinion and social policy: a research review' Journal of Social Policy. 5, 1975, 19-32.

10. Fischer, J. The Effectiveness of Social Casework. Springfield, I11., Charles C. Thomas, 1976.

11. Fischer, J. 'Does anything work?' Journal of Social Service Research. 1 (3) Spring 1978, 215-43.

12.. Rees, S. Social Work Face to Face. London, Edward Arnold, 1978.

13. Rees, S. & Emerson, A. Disabled Children Disabling Policies. Sydney, S.W.R.C. Monograph No. 35, 1983.

14. Galtung, J. Theory and Method in Social Science. London, Allen and Unwin, 1967.

15. Page, R. & Clark, G.A. Who Cares? London, National Children's Bureau, 1977.

16. Royal Commission into New South Wales Prisons (Chairman: The Honourable Mr Justice Nagle) Sydney, 1978.

17. Goldberg, E. Helping the Aged. London, Allen & Unwin, 1970.

18. Rubenstein, H. & Bloch, M.G. 'Helping clients who are poor: worker and client perceptions of problems, activities and outcomes' Social Service Review. 52 (1) 1978, 69-84.

19. Timms, N. The Receiving End. London, Routledge and Kegan Paul, 1973.

20. McCoy, T., Penich, E.C., Powell, J. & Read, M.R. 'Clients' reactions to an outreach program' Social Work. 20 (6) 1975, 442-4.

21. Powell, B.J., Shaw, D. & O'Neil, C. 'Client evaluations of a clinic's services' Hospital and Community Psychiatry. 22 June 1971, 189-190.

22. Bedfordshire Social Services Department, Handicapped Children. 1978.

23. Sainsbury, E. Social Work with Families. London, Routledge, 1975.

24. McKinlay, J.B. 'Some approaches and problems in the study of the use of services' Journal of Health and Social Behaviour. 13, June 1975.

25. Reid, W.M. 'Characteristics of casework intervention' Welfare in Review. Vol. 5, No. 8, 1967.

26. MaKay, A., Goldberg, E.M. & Fruin, D.J. 'Consumers and a social services department' Social Work Today. 4 (16) 1973.

27. Cohen, A. 'Consumer view: retarded mothers and the social services' Social Work Today. 1 (12) 1971, 35-43.

28. Robinson, T. In Worlds Apart. London, Bedford Square Press, 1978.

29. Truax, C. & Carkhuff, R. Towards Effective Counselling and Psychotherapy. Chicago, Aldine, 1967.

30. Sheldon, B. 'Social work effectiveness experiments: review and implications', British Journal of Social Work, (16) pp. 223-242, 1986.

31. Fisher, M., Newton, C., and Sainsbury E., Mental Health Social Work Observed, London, Allen and Unwin, 1984.

32. Liffman, M., Power for the Poor, Sydney, Allen and Unwin, 1979.

Illuminative Evaluation

Maureen Buist

INTRODUCTION

The qualitative research approach known as illuminative evaluation developed from educational researchers' dissatisfaction with the failure of traditional experimental research methods to take account of the situations which they were investigating. An early criticism was that in experimental research, the emphasis was on the strict control of variables but this was rarely possible in the real world where laboratory conditions could not be replicated. Thus the only way in which the necessary objectivity could be achieved was through random sampling which was an expensive and time consuming exercise. Moreover as Stenhouse [1] points out, a study of samples involves the assumption that the treatment has been consistent throughout. This is something which we cannot take for granted in real life; it does not always happen that new forms of practice are consistently applied. Sinclair and Shaw [2], for example, who undertook an experimental study of case work in a prison setting found that prison welfare officers actually gave fewer interviews than had been agreed initially.

Further, Stenhouse [1] argues that, as control of purity is impossible in social research, a random sample is almost inevitable which means that the results will be made in terms of statistical probabilities. This provides a pointer or guide on how best to act and as such is perfectly acceptable in the experimental sciences where we have, for example, no particular regard for the way in which a particular seed of corn or battery hen has responded to the application of a particular treatment, but are only interested in the aggregate effect on the total population. Unfortunately the opposite is the case in the social sciences where the individual is our concern. Here we are not in a position to say that because a treatment is most successful with sixty percent of sample the other forty percent do not matter.

These arguments can be applied to the methodological approach of Gibbons [3] who attempted to test the hypothesis that a specially organised social work service using a task centred approach would have a more favourable impact on the personal and social circumstances of people who had attempted suicide by self-poisoning, than the normally available service. The authors selected a control and treatment group of clients and looked at the outcome in terms of six criteria. Although they were able to form some conclusions on the basis of their data, they were left with more unanswered than answered questions and they could only postulate the structural relationships between the problem and their findings. Their project highlights the difficulties encountered in attempting to reach the level of control necessary when carrying out a research project in real life situations using experimental methods.

Goldberg and Connelly [4], who acknowledge some of the difficulties inherent in carrying out social research by experimental methods, propose a solution of introducing cross sectional comparisons. Their answer to the problem of identifying the most successful outcomes of treatment programmes is to note the characteristics of the client group and then look at a range of different regimes and treatments at the same time. They suggest that this will reveal the links between input and outcomes. However, these attempts to adjust experimental methods to the conditions of the real world are still unable to take account of the kind of changes over time which inevitably occur as practitioners re-adjust and re-organise their methods to meet the demands of the practical context.

While qualitative research methods may be selected in preference to experimental research methods on utilitarian grounds, others have chosen this particular approach on ideological grounds. Over the last thirty years perspectives on understanding social phenomena have tended towards either positivism or a more naturalistic or humanistic viewpoint. Broadly the former is concerned with the objective and causal and raises questions about imputs and outputs and the latter is concerned with understanding subjective experience and the focus is processes. In this perspective the aim is to explain and understand what is taking place. The research procedures which are chosen are ones which provide understanding of social structure and process from the participant's point of view [5]. Several theories exist within this framework among which symbolic interactionism, phenomenology and ethnomethodology are the best known. There have been many studies from an interactionist perspective using participant and non-participant observation among which the classical examples are Becker [6] on student culture in a medical school and Cicourel and Kitsuse [7] on the counselling of high school students, but these studies were often somewhat protracted affairs. Becker's study involved two years field work and took around ten years to emerge in print by which time, as the author himself admitted, the situation had no doubt changed.

Moreover, some qualitative studies have been criticised for being little more than descriptive accounts of processes; they did not explore the reasons why people behaved in particular ways in particular contexts. Through their neglect of the socio-historical contexts in which meanings were created they did not promote understanding. Consequently studies of this nature were regarded as insufficiently responsive to the type of demands made on researchers, particularly those involved in the evaluation of innovatory programmes where there was a requirement to clarify and interpret the programme for decision makers and practitioners within a limited time scale. It was in response to the recognition that both traditional experimental and qualitative research methods were inadequate for the task of evaluating educational innovations that the approach known as illuminative evaluation, in which the primary concern was description and interpretation rather than measurement and prediction, was developed [8].

METHODOLOGICAL STRATEGIES

In a monograph outlining the methodological strategies of illuminative evaluation and its application to educational practice, Parlett and Hamilton [9] begin by explaining two concepts which are central to the method. The first is the 'instructional system' by which the authors mean the variety of formalised plans contained within prospectuses and statements about the innovation. They suggest that from a study of these documents the researcher will learn details of the syllabus, pedagogic assumptions and teaching styles. The parallel of the instructional system in social work would be the outline of the planned programme, theories in social work upon which the practice would be based and the social work methods which would be applied. However, as the authors point out, taking account of the instructional system means only that the researcher will be in possession of the idealised specification or blue print of the innovation. The researcher's task is then to study the implementation of the innovation in context.

The second concept is the 'learning milieu'. This is the context of the school and covers the social, psychological and material environment in which students and teachers work. It is through recognising the interaction of pressures, customs, opinions and work styles which suffuse the teaching and learning, or in social work, the social work practice and client response, that the researcher comes to understand what is taking place.

Parlett and Hamilton [9] describe illuminative evaluation as a general research strategy which aims to be both adaptable and eclectic and thus argue that the choice of research tactics should be based upon the problem undergoing examination.

They suggest three stages in field work within which data is collected via observation, interview, questioning and, if appropriate, tests. Documentary and background sources are also consulted.

During the exploratory stage the researcher notes recurring trends and issues which are of central concern, 'key issues', and builds up a record of what is taking place, listening to the assumptions being made and watching the interpersonal relationships which exist. Examples might be noting whether staff in old people's homes knock before entering a client's bedroom or the physical arrangements in an approved school and the way in which the building is used. The researcher also has discussions with participants to test out and elaborate on her observations.

The next stage of field work involves interviewing a random selection of participants to obtain their views on the key issues involved in the innovation being studied. In the course of these interviews questions are raised based on the awareness and knowledge which the researcher has accumulated in the earlier stage. The researcher must have established rapport with participants, adhere to fairly strict procedures and take care not to pre-dispose answers. This process of progressive focusing is common to nearly all qualitative research approaches including ethnography [10]. It is at this stage that the original research problem may be developed and transformed, so much so that the researcher ends up tackling issues very different from those which she started out with.

The third stage consists of seeking general principles underlying the operation of the practice and looking for links which explain what is going on. Parlett and Hamilton [9] are at pains to explain that the three stages are to some extent indistinct. It is a process of sorting out the wood from the trees. The authors also suggest that the researcher's conclusions be tested out by the introduction of specially prepared questionnaires based upon the researcher's knowledge of the situation and, where appropriate, attitude, personality and achievement tests may be administered and their results integrated with the study's findings.

EXAMPLES FROM THE LITERATURE

Although studies of social work practice using illuminative evaluation as such are rare, several use qualitative methods in a somewhat similar manner. In a case study of a community home for girls Ackland [11] who used both interviews and participant observation, sought to discover the impact of a change of policy from one in which the emphasis was on social training and control to another in which the emphasis was on individual care and treatment. Prior to beginning his study he examined the 'blue print'. The establishment was to change from an approved school in which great value had been placed upon adherence to rules with the aim of rehabilitation, to a community home in which the intention was to foster a flexible treatment approach with opportunities for personal autonomy and growth. It was not until Ackland had begun his period of observation that the issues on which his study was eventually to focus emerged. For example, his realisation that home leave (which was regarded as a significant factor in the treatment process) had been incorporated into a control system, in which a home visit was a reward for good behaviour, led him to concentrate his study on the issues of control, staff/girl relationships and the girls' treatment; i.e. he eventually concentrated not on the outcome of the new regime but the actual practice.

In a study of the efficacy of social work practice, Maluccio [12] explored what it is that makes for effective interpersonal helping in social work or related disciplines. He wanted to identify the factors which contributed to the effectiveness of service delivery and chose a qualitative approach because of his dissatisfaction with previous research which had attempted to understand the client/social worker relationship in a linear manner and which failed to acknowledge the many factors which impinge in social encounters. He began by taking account of the context in which social work/client encounters took place. Interviews with social workers and clients focussed on the similarities and dissimilarities of the views of the two groups and their perceptions and expectations of the service. His aim was to identify the key issues in the situation and the part they played in the outcome of the social work/client encounters. As a former practitioner he was already aware that the client's expectations were a key issue as far as the delivery of the service was concerned but he discovered that another key issue was the social workers' expectations of what was being offered. Interviews with social workers revealed that some clearly expressed a need for human involvement in the course of their work and when, for example, the client did not also seek this but merely stated what he required, some workers were dissatisfied with the encounter.

Maluccio also identified that several features in the agency context such as the role played by the receptionist and the connections which the agency held with outside agencies also played a part in client satisfaction. In addition to qualitative data Maluccio collected demographic and other social economic data on clients in order to expand understanding of the qualitative findings of the study.

In a project using the methodological approach of illuminative evaluation Ferri [13] set out to assess a new type of nursery centre which combined education and social service provision for pre-school children. She began by looking at the 'blue print' for the new service and established that the aim was to offer high quality day care and nursery education in a single unit. The ideas had proved attractive on two counts; a comprehensive approach to meeting the needs of the under fives was regarded as best and it was economically more viable than dual provision. Ferri began by observing what took place in the combined centres and found that there were differences in the amount and nature of staff interaction with children. Teaching staff were more involved in educational tasks and nursery nurses in caring tasks. Interviews with participants revealed that staff perceived the children differently on the basis of the type of place which the child held; full-time places being allocated to children by social services and part-time places by the heads of the centres.

Moreover, relations between teaching staff and nursery nurses were less than harmonious owing to discrepancies between salary levels and working conditions. There was a tendency for teachers to view themselves as educational experts and the nursery nurses to view themselves as care experts. Thus in practice separate and not integrated concepts of care and education pertained in the centres.

Testing of the cognitive and social/emotional development of the children revealed that those in the centres made better progress than their peers in day nurseries. The author points out that this finding alone offers little insight into what factors account for the difference and that it is only through the inclusion of qualitative data (such as the observation that children in the centre spent more time in educational activities than their counterparts in day nurseries) that we begin to understand how outcomes are produced.

METHODOLOGICAL ISSUES

Among the many methodological issues in qualitative research is the problem of the selection of key issues; which issue to highlight with the possibility that the researcher may be biased or that the evidence does not support the choice. It should perhaps be pointed out that the problem of the subjectivity of the researcher is not peculiar to qualitative research. Research by any method requires judgement at some stage in the selection of the problem for investigation, the choice of sample, selection and construction of tests and in the relative weight given to results in the selection of the presentation of findings.

As to the question of selection of key issues, several authors suggest methods for imposing a structured framework on the data. The main aim of each of these strategies is to impose order on the sheer mass of data which has been accumulated and to ensure that the evidence is there to back up the researchers' statements.

Schatzman and Strauss [14] propose one way of deciding what should be focussed on: to make notes during observation of events which appear to be important to the situation being studied. By documenting these the researcher will develop an awareness of issues which he should be in a position to check through. They suggest putting information from interviews on cards so that it is possible to move the data about. In this way what they call 'classes' of data may emerge and be recognised.

A more recent method of dealing with qualitative data acquired through interviews comes from Bliss et al [15], who take descriptive categories as they begin to emerge from inspection of the data and then organise them into well defined description language. The system uses a notation derived from systems linguistics; this sets out category names in a way which shows their interdependencies. The authors claim the system is flexible and that it generates network-like structures in which it is possible to identify which categories belong with others, which are interdependent and which are conditional on the choice of others. Stenhouse [1] who prefers the term evidence to data, goes so far as to say that the evidence from case studies, field notes and interview tapes, should be stored and accessible to any researcher who wishes to subject it to critical assessment. Nevertheless, it is likely that bias may occur but only in the extent to which a researcher focusses on one issue rather than another; it is in the choice and not necessarily truth of issues that variations occurs. Parlett and Hamilton [9] suggest involving fellow researchers in carrying out an independent analysis of the data and, if necessary, challenging the preliminary interpretation of this. Hammersley and Atkinson [10] suggest adopting respondent validation, by which they mean allowing the participants to comment on the accuracy of the researchers' portrayal of the situation. Some researchers hold seminars at which they invite participants' comments.

It is practice such as this and the fact that qualitative research recognises the concerns and views of both high and low status participants that make this research style a more democratic one than experimental research. However, one implication of this style is that the question of whose view of a situation should predominate can arise as it often happens that the most powerful individuals in a project may consider that their views should be given most weight. This issue is best tackled at the outset by explaining to participants that the perceptions of each group will be recognised. Ackland [11] points out how frequently the presentation in reports of the views and perceptions of low status individuals such as children or inmates has been taken as measures of their attitudes and outlooks and thus indicators of their reaction to the treatment they are supposed to be receiving rather than authentic and valid alternative definitions of the regimes to which they were exposed.

There is, however, a possibility that in allowing the reader access to respondents' views, they become much more exposed and consequently more vulnerable. This poses ethical problems for the researcher. Macdonald [16] argues that respondents should not only be assured of confidentiality but also be given control over the use of the data' they should be shown the final report and their agreement sought before it is submitted to the funders. Others disagree with this view and say that the researcher should make clear to respondents at the outset what the aims of the study are and who is to receive the report. Even where this view is subscribed to most researchers who carry out qualitative research would accept they have a moral duty not to expose respondents and where it appeared vital to include particular data to seek alternative means to doing so which did not put individuals at risk.

It is often stated that one of the major disadvantages of a qualitative approach is the fact that the findings cannot be generalised in the same way as the results of experimental research.

One way round this is to undertake a study similar to that recently completed of library access and sixth form study [17], which looked at twenty-four institutions. The case studies were carried out by independent researchers, but the use of multiple settings makes generalisation more possible.

The researchers were interested in the use of libraries by sixth formers who were undertaking A-levels in a range of types of schools. The main issue upon which the project focussed was whether A-level courses promoted intellectual independence.

The researchers accumulated knowledge about the teaching and learning through interviews with teachers, students and librarians and supplemented this with information on budget allocation, staffing levels, book stocks and the amount of staff time spent with students. Their main conclusions were that although sixth formers come to take responsibility for organising their work few become independent learners. Interviews revealed students rarely consult sources other than teachers or text books.

It is not difficult to draw a parallel from the conduct of this study (involving independent but similar research of several institutions) to the way in which issues in social work could be tackled.

Ultimately, since the primary task of illuminative evaluation is description and interpretation in context it should be recognised that this offers decision makers and practitioners the opportunity to apply their own professional judgement in taking account of and applying findings elsewhere. Moreover because research within this framework takes note both of variables and the mechanisms or processes which link them in a given context, the opportunity is there for the generation of theoretical insights and new concepts.

As we saw earlier illuminative evaluation, although essentially interpretative, does not entirely exclude quantifiable aspects. Ideally the output of a research project carried out in this way should be revealing, useful and intelligible to those involved and provide them with insight into the problems which they themselves recognise. Although it will not fully resolve the issues which cause concern, it should at least illuminate.

References

1. Stenhouse, L. 'The Study of Samples and the Study of Cases' British Educational Research Journal. Vol. 6, No. 1, 1980.
2. Sinclair, I.A.C., Shaw, M.J. & Troup, E.J. 'The relationship between introversion and response to case work in a prison setting' British Journal of Social and Clinical Psychology. 13, 1974, 51-60.
3. Gibbons, J. 'An evaluation of the effectiveness of social work intervention using task centred methods after deliberate self poisoning' in Godlberg, E.M. & Connelly, N. (Eds.) Evaluative Research in Social Care. Heinemann, 1980 [4].
4. Goldberg, E.M. & Connelly, N. Evaluative Research in Social Care. Heinemann, 1980.
5. Bulmer, M. Sociological Research Methods. The Macmillan Press, 1983.
6. Becker, H.S. Boys in White: Student Culture in a Medical School. University of Chicago Press, 1961.
7. Cicourel, A.V. & Kitsuse, J.I. The Educational Decision-Makers. Bobbs-Merrill, Indianapolis, 1963.
8. Parlett, M. & King, J.G. Concentrated Study. Research in Higher Education Monograph, No. 14. London, Society for Research in Higher Education, 1971.
9. Parlett, M. & Hamilton, D. Evaluation as Illumination. A new approach to the study of innovatory programs. Centre for Research in the Educational Sciences, University of Edinburgh Occasional Paper, No. 9, 1972.
10. Hammersley, M. & Atkinson, P. Ethnography: Principles in Practice. Tavistock Publications, 1983.
11. Ackland, J.W. Girls in Care: A Case Study of Residential Treatment. Gower, 1982.
12. .Maluccio, A.N. Learning from Clients. The Free Press, New York, 1979.
13. Ferri, E. 'Evaluating Combined Nursery Centres' In Goldberg, E.M. & Connelly, N. (Eds.) Evaluative Research in Social Care. Heinemann, 1980 [4].
14. Schatzman, L. & Strauss, A. Field Research. Strategies for a Natural Sociology. Prentice-Hall, 1973.

15. Bliss, J., Monk, M. & Ogborn, J. Systematic Networks: A new approach. Forthcoming.

16. MacDonald, B. 'Evaluation and Control of Education' in Innovation, Evaluation, Research and the Problem of Control. Safari Interim Paper, Centre for Applied Research in Education, University of East Anglia, 1974.

17. Riddoch, J. & Hopkins, D. The Sixth Form and Libraries: Problems of access to knowledge. To be published by the British Library R & D Department early next year. LIR report No. 24. The archive is housed at the Centre for Applied Research in Education, University of East Anglia.

Group-Controlled Experiments in the Evaluation of Social Work Services

Brian Sheldon

Between 1972 and 1976 two American reviews of experimental research into the outcome of social work services [1] [2] [3] were published. Here are their conclusions:

> 'The researchers for many reasons were rarely able to conclude that a programme had even modest success in achieving its major goals' [1].
>
> 'How could this incredible situation have come about? The bulk of practitioners in an entire profession appear, at worst, to be practising in ways that are not helpful or are even detrimental to their clients, and at best, operating without a shred of empirical evidence validating their efforts' [3].

Thus, while in Britain the employment market for social workers was booming following the implementation of the Seebohm Report, and the number of students leaving training was peaking at around 3500 C.Q.S.W.s per year, in the United States increasingly strident critical voices were being raised questioning the value of such services.

The research analysed in these two reviews falls into two different patterns:

1) experiments with non-intervention controls
2) experiments with other-treated controls or with 'defector' controls (see Figs 1, 2 and 3 respectively).

The design of experiments with non-intervention control groups is straightforward (in a procedural sense – if not in practice).

The aim is to select two representative groups of clients who are as much like each other as possible, except that one group will receive social work services and the

FIGURE 1

Basic Experimental Design with a Non-Intervention Control Group

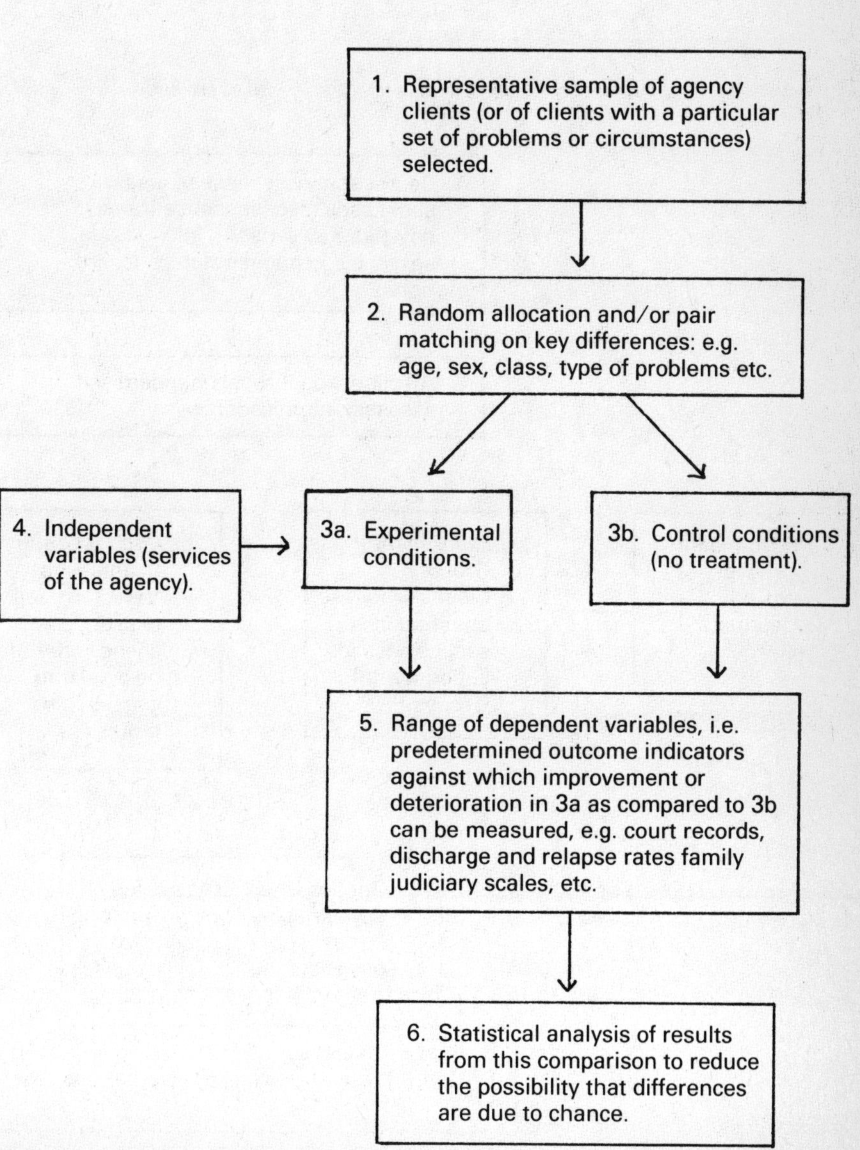

other will not. Clients may either be specifically matched on a number of key variables and then allocated one to each group, or, given a large enough sample, clients can be randomly allocated to the experimental and control groups, so spreading the possibilities that any potentially confounding variables will be as likely to be found in one group as the other.

FIGURE 2

Experimental Designs with 'Defector' Control Group

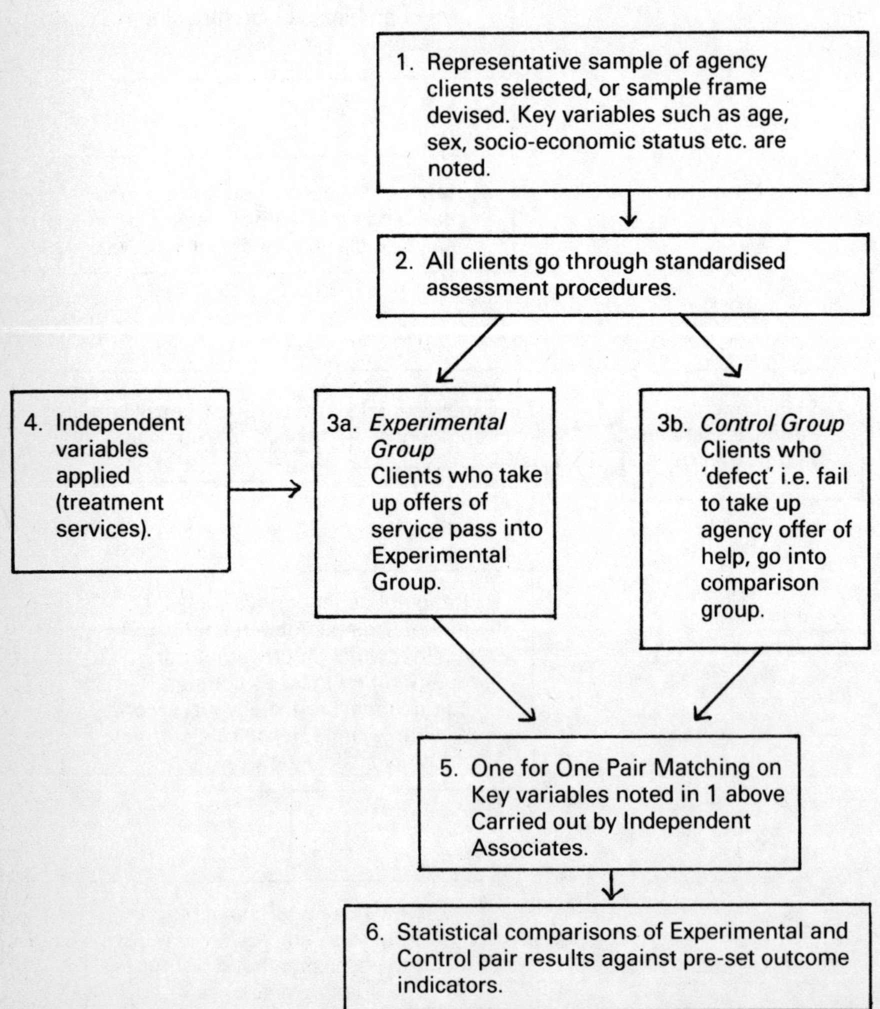

'Defector Control' studies have the advantage that they do not raise the ethical issues associated with the deliberate withholding of services from clients. However, careful analysis is required to ensure that the 'drop out' clients are comparable with the clients who decide to use the services of the agency. They may be less motivated to overcome their problems, which would mean a built-in advantage for experimental group results, or the reverse could be true, in that the assessment procedures common to all subjects might be enough to settle certain problems for the more intelligent clients. These clients might then drop out, and present as a formidable level of 'spontaneous remission' for the experimental-group workers to try to improve upon. Careful analysis can expose these differences to some extent, but it has not always been done. The study by Levitt, Beiser and Robertson [4] provides a good example of this approach. In this study of child guidance services there were no significant differences between 'drop out' and full-service families.

Experiments with other-treated controls attempt to compare the efficacy of two possible approaches to the problems of a typical sample of clients. Probably the most famous examples of this approach are:

(i) the work of Reid and Shyne [5] who compared brief, time-limited, task-centred casework methods with the established long-term open-ended approach;

(ii) Goldberg's study 'Helping the Aged' [6] where the effects of services provided to elderly people in the community by trained project workers were compared with the regular services of experienced but unqualified local authority Welfare Department workers.

Stark choices from the failure of the established and the distinctive methods of the profession to stand up to this kind of scientific scrutiny – not once or twice, but on many occasions.

Logically, the profession and its training institutions ought to have felt compelled to decide whether;

1) to abandon, or at least seriously question their attachment to:

   (a) most kinds of social casework;
   (b) certain styles of groupwork;
   (c) relationship and 'interview therapies' in general;
   (d) psychodynamically-derived procedures in particular;
   (e) Much of the work hitherto done to prevent delinquency;

or

FIGURE 3

Experimental Design with Other-treated Control Group

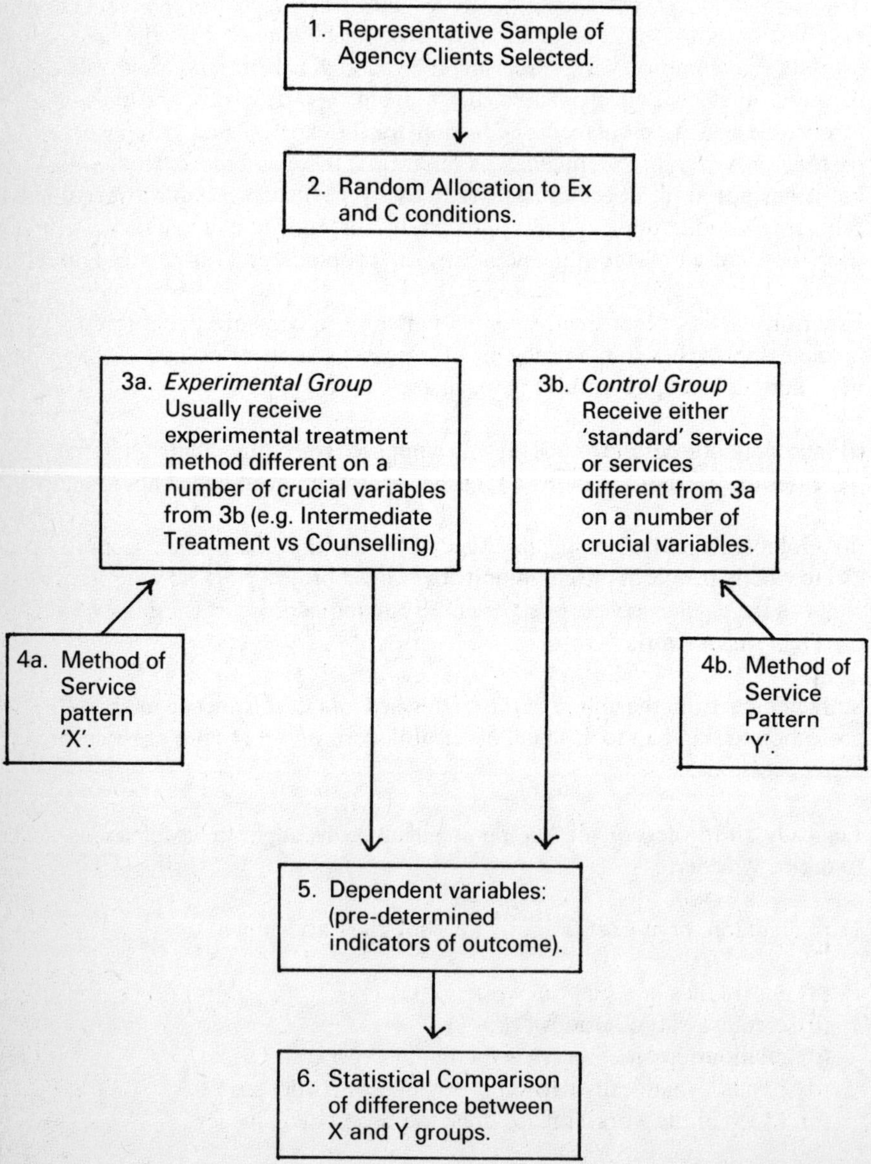

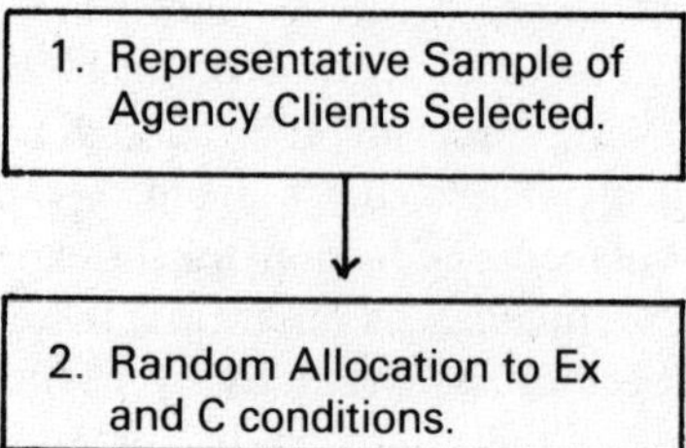

1. Representative Sample of Agency Clients Selected.
2. Random Allocation to Ex and C conditions.
3a. *Experimental Group* Usually receive experimental treatment method different on a number of crucial variables from 3b (e.g. Intermediate Treatment vs Counselling)
3b. *Control Group* Receive either 'standard' service or services different from 3a on a number of crucial variables.
4a. Method of Service pattern 'X'.
4b. Method of Service Pattern 'Y'.
5. Dependent variables: (pre-determined indicators of outcome).
6. Statistical Comparison of difference between X and Y groups.

2) to renounce the rather-compromised position of scientific respectability earned through association with the social sciences, and through the work of a few pioneers, during the preceding forty odd years [5] [6] [7] [8] [9].

But professions resemble large oil tankers in the time it takes them to alter course, and Social Work's reaction to the evidence from controlled experimentation, has been no exception to this rule.* What reasons are there for this delay?

Our discipline still occupies what Kuhn [11] would call a preparadigmatic stage of development. That is, as practitioners, supervisors, researchers, course-syllabus writers and teachers, we have not yet arrived at a roughly-agreed set of criteria against which theoretical propositions and research findings can be assessed and either temporarily accepted, or placed on 'hold' pending further work, or rejected as untenable [12]. Therefore, any arguments we have about the believability of ideas and evidence, and their implications, tend quickly to become ideological ones; at best they become philosophical.

There is little scope for dialogue or a decisive contest of ideas, and no basis for a consensus within which we might steadily improve our performance in training students and in selecting and testing out ideas to improve the quality of services. Courses, agencies and teams often operate as isolated little city states, each with their own interesting banners and customs. In some lights this may look like an inspiring diversity of views, but a closer, cooler look might reveal that it results from a low rate of disciplinary development. A good example of this is the way in which the research literature – particularly the effectiveness and consumer opinion literature – is used. Some courses teach little or nothing on these matters at all. Many social workers and their managers appear to regard topics such as research and evaluation as something they are innoculated with by academics; one shot is supposed to last out a career in the field!

We are equally in danger of neglecting the development of institutions capable of disseminating the lessons of effectiveness and consumer research, sharing in the problems of operationalisation and encouraging routine service-evaluation in the field. The obvious choice for this two-way 'pumping station' role are Research and Forward Planning Sections of Local Authority Social Services Departments. But as Bowl and Fuller [13] suggest, they are presently preoccupied with other predominantly in-house organisational matters – whether through choice, or by reasons of political or bureaucratic pressure, is unknown.

---

* A parallel can be drawn here with the slow reaction of Psychiatry to studies pointing to the very large placebo element present in ECT procedures [10].

A third set of reasons for delay stems from the fact that there is a major problem regarding estimates of the likely relevance of evaluation research findings to any given aspect of social work. Despite a number of academic attempts [14] [15], and (in Britain) a series of policy initiatives, the long-awaited consolidation of the social worker's role in society seems as elusive as ever [16] [17]. The range and scope of our functions and the number of different interpretations of the priority-order in which these should be considered, continues to expand.

Therefore, with evaluation experiments still largely in the hands of a few academics and research personnel, it seems inevitable that this process will continue to resemble taking flashlight pictures of a broad, dark landscape.

It has further been argued [18] that the predominantly American findings reviewed by Fischer [3] are of little relevance to British social work, since they are the product of another culture, another pattern of services, another way of doing things. Normally the argument rests there, so that acceptance or rejection of the chastening message of US research depends upon one's knowledge or accepted prejudices regarding what goes on over there. A more profitable line is to examine the original work. When this is done some of the more popular stereotypes collapse. Take for example the widespread view that the American social workers featured in such studies tend to concentrate their services on the insight-hungry middle classes. In fact, of the seventeen experiments reviewed by Fischer, eight sought to evaluate delinquency prevention schemes; the next largest target group we would call multi-problem families; the next, studies of child guidance services; and there follows a small scatter of individual studies concerned with, for example, the problems of young blacks [19] [20], the elderly mentally infirm [21] and the problems of women married to alcoholics [22]. Only one study in Fischer's sample supports the British prejudice, Most's study [23] of marital work with young, white, middle class women. In most of these studies the social workers appear to be working with the institutions and in the places relevant to their clients' problems, in homes, schools, settlements, neighbourhoods and on the streets, and not just in the office [8] [24] [25].

Similar attacks have often been mounted on the suitability of the outcome indicators used in these experiments for the kind of methods typically employed by social workers, and for the complex problems that confront them. The main line of argument here is that social work, by its very nature, represents a broad-scope intervention in broad-scope problems, and that experimental methodology, by its very nature, 'squeezes out' or 'compresses' important outcome data – particularly qualitative data – by relying on binary type, 'yes or no', 'greater or lesser', 'present or not present' indicators. These methodological arguments will be addressed in more detail later. It is sufficient to assert here that this is just not true of the first generation of American experiments. In thirteen of the seventeen studies reviewed by Fischer there is a strong qualitative component. Clients and their families are followed up and interviewed about their views of progress or determination. Behaviour rating scales are also used, and standardised scales of family functioning are applied pre and post intervention.

Turning to the input side of the American experiments, far more serious problems face us. These mainly concern the clear identification of independent variables, and hence, the representativeness of this work. In a number of the studies reviewed by Mullen and Dumpson [1] and by Fischer [2] [3] we have only a shadowy idea of what the independent variables actively consisted of – that is, of what was done that was intended to help. For example, in Behling's study of work with families on relief [26], the 'intensive casework' input is further defined as: 'services rendered to a small caseload (about fifty cases – roughly half the size of the usual public assistance load), given to two hundred public assistance cases over a fifteen month period'. A control group received the normal services of the agency. In other words, some clients got the regular services of the agency (whatever they were) and some got a more 'intense' burst of regular agency services. We know little more than that about what in this particular experiment seemed to work quite well! In seven of the experiments reviewed by Fischer it was not possible to say what was being tested with any certainty at all [20] [22] [23]. In a large number of the original research documents we are given little more than labels and definitions of the type of service provided, with little information on the way workers understood and interpreted the relevant theories; what they saw as their main methods and objectives; what key behaviours were associated with these understandings, plans, goals and preferences; what the clients felt themselves to be receiving – and what they made of it. This conclusion will bear repeating: in a substantial number of the American evaluation experiments we have only a limited idea of what it is that appears not to work.

How did we get into this embarassing situation? It is common for critics of effectiveness research to blame the strictures of the experimental approach for this problem because of the way it tends to concentrate the minds of researchers on the problems of determining outcome. Indeed, it is quite common for this entire body of less-than-encouraging results to be seen as largely an artifact of distorting pressures present in this methodological pattern [27] [28]. Let us now examine this methodological approach stage by stage, and in this way assess both its general usefulness to social work research, and in particular whether there is any truth in the allegation reported above.

PROBLEMS OF EXPERIMENTAL RESEARCH

Experimental methods provide the strictest test of therapeutic good intent in any discipline and clear negative results tell us much. In the physical sciences they have a very important standing indeed, because research there tends to be focused more on well-recognised 'barriers to further progress' [29].

Why in social work do the issues get so personalised? The catalogue of failures associated with research into biochemical factors in schizophrenia (which may well exist nonetheless) or the equivocal literature on the reliability of psychiatric diagnoses [31] [32] do not lead to popular calls for less public investment in psychiatry, nor even for re-distribution of certain of that profession's functions. But this is often the reaction to negative findings in social work research [33]. Partly this has to do with public ambivalence about our cause and to the comparative newness of this profession. But mainly it stems from the fact that it is very difficult in social work to distinguish between service and service providers. In social work research (particularly in the way it has been conducted hitherto) the social workers themselves (not particularly drugs or isolated therapeutic procedures) are the independent variables. Negative results then imply not just the failure of the method but also of the social worker.

The use of social workers themselves as undifferentiated independent variables also raises the spectre of the 'therapist uniformity myth' from psychotherapy research. In experimental studies the assumption is that just as client differences get averaged-out by random allocation to experimental or control conditions, the differences between the different workers' styles and theoretical preferences get similarly randomised among the different subjects. There is evidence from psychological research that clients respond as much to the styles and manner of their would-be-helpers as they do to their methods per se [34] [35]. Indeed it is likely (subject to some arguments about the precise nature of the key personal variables [36]) that while some helpers seem to be able to help across a range of social and psychological difficulties some fail to engage their clients at all and are virtually inert, and others actually produce deleterious effects. A worsening of problems in the experimental group is not at all uncommon in this type of research [27] [37]. The assumption that social worker styles are randomised and may be treated as uniform masks these interpersonal differences. Experimental investigations of social work effectiveness may well contain hidden clusters of useful results which cancel out to zero in later statistical comparisons.

Because of the initial preference for 'black box'* physics-type experimentation, not only do we know little of the nature of the input in terms of its rough similarity or otherwise to practice elsewhere, we also know little or nothing about the manner in which services were delivered and the reaction of particular clients to particular approaches. We do know, however, that studies which seek to match clients and workers tend to produce more positive results [38]. Not having this information on the process of attempts to help means that we are not in a position to select out and reinforce specific therapeutic practices; particular approaches to service delivery, or styles of work associated with effectiveness and client satisfaction. Clearly in the future we need a more detailed approach to the input side of experimental studies, and more attention to individual results. We already have experience of this type of approach in a related form of research – the consumer-reaction study. This detailed, 'natural history' approach to the study of services and their consumers is well-developed in the work of Sainsbury and Nixon [39], Rees and Wallace [40] and Mayer and Timms [41]. Although there is nothing unfair about 'black box' experimental methodology, we could learn more if the studies were less experimental *contests* and more experimental investigation.

However, a second set of problems exists which is more fundamental. It concerns the difficulty most agencies have over random allocation to non-intervention or even to 'service-delay' groups. The preponderance of American effectiveness studies is due in part to their early and substantial investment in social work education but also to the particular pattern of services they have developed. Their enormous range of voluntary, private and public grant-aided agencies means that groups of social workers have regularly to justify their own existence and make comparisons between their own services and those provided by similar bodies nearby. This gives much American social work a 'project' quality: things have to be achieved and demonstrated to outside bodies within a particular time scale. The embodiment of British services within the framework of the welfare state, although preferable to this author in most respects, has tended to emphasise continuity of service and the need for evenhandedness of provision, rather than specialisation, distinctiveness and competition. Indeed it is difficult to imagine many of the classic social work experiments taking place in British Social Services Departments.

Nevertheless there have been some excellent British experiments. Goldberg's study [6] of the outcome of different patterns of service to the elderly, Folkard's work [42] on intensive versus 'traditional' probation methods; Shaw's study [43] of social work in prison and the clear-sighted study of Gibbons et al [44] on task-centred

* The analogy is drawn from early experiments in atomic physics where the properties of new elements were inferred by subjecting them to bombardment in a 'black box' and observing how the energy was changed as it re-emerged. The precise goings on inside the 'black box' were a mystery.

methods in cases of deliberate self-poisoning, stand out as examples. But these pieces of research either take advantage of rarely-occurring 'natural' experimental situations (as when there is a changeover in the pattern of service-delivery) or they take place in very specialised settings. Folkard's Home Office Research Unit study is the nearest thing to an exception to this rule, but, like the Goldberg study, the other-treated design cannot tell us anything about what would have happened had the probation officers been able to stay away altogether. Although random assignment to a non-intervention condition always raises some ethical problems, in Britain's predominantly statutory, priority conscious, risk-oriented welfare services, these are amplified and augmented by a host of other practical and legal difficulties.

The ethical problems referred to above, can be addressed by arguing that:

(i) Although 'doing our clients no harm' might be the first ethical priority, doing

TABLE 1

Special and Comparison Groups by Background Variables at First Assessment (Percentage distribution)

Variables		Special Group (N = 150)	Comparison Group (N = 150)
Age:	Under 80 years	56	53
	80 and over	44	47
Marital state:	Single	15	11
	Married	22	15
	Widowed	60	71
	Divorced/separated	3	3
	No evidence	–	–
Sex:	Male	32	21
	Female	68	79
Social Class:	I, II, III non manual	11	15
	III manual	37	36
	IV and V	49	43
	No evidence	3	6
Living Group:	Lives alone	64	65
	Does not live alone	36	35

(Source: Goldberg, 1970 [6])

them some good must run a close second, and a third must be improving services through feedback on results and the fostering of a healthy spirit of consumerism;

(ii) All services contain hidden opportunity costs; if we are wasting money on certain ineffective or inefficient types of intended help, then we have less to spend elsewhere where it could be made to count. These are particularly strong arguments in the case of social work where, until recently, studies showing clear effectiveness were rather more the exception than the rule.

A further set of problems arising in experimental research concern the adequacy of control arrangements. Ideally, two conditions are required: first, that following random allocation, the two groups should not be imbalanced in respect of factors such as age, gender, type of problem, socio-economic status, and so forth. Table 1 provides an example of successful matching, but it should be noted that not all studies achieve this and so endless statistical arguments ensue over results.

Here is the matching process at work:

> 'Had the random method of allocation been effective in producing two reasonably matched groups? We compared the two initial groups each containing 150 clients on basic variables, such as age, marital state, sex, social class and living group. On the whole they turned out to be reasonably similar. The table above shows that the groups were well matched on age, whether they were living alone and reasonably matched on social class. However, there were 11 per cent more widowed old persons in the comparison group (just below significance level) and 11 per cent more men in the special group (just above the level of significance). This was unfortunate. If the whole procedure of random allocation had been carried out on a hundred different samples of old people, a result such as this with more men in the special group, would only have occured in five samples. The question now arises whether this difference in sex distribution was likely to lead to a distortion in our final results.' [6]

Although random allocation and close matching bring their headaches, these procedures are an essential ingredient of experimental research. In one of the first studies of social work ever conducted [8] two thirds of the experimental group of children assessed as being at risk of juvenile delinquency were rated as having 'substantially benefitted' from contact with social workers, but on comparison with the control group children this favourable result evaporated; the untreated controls had improved to the same extent [35] [45]. Control groups make possible a comparison between specialised, well-focused professional help and the randomly-distributed advice and succour available to us all in our everyday lives, but there may be a case for a much closer investigation of what happens to control group subjects. In most experiments they are treated as so much dead meat, when in fact the natural 'ecology' of the control group and support received through contact with other professionals, non-professional helpers and informal aid groups, to say nothing of sensible friends and relatives. I am not arguing here that social work should not do better on average, rather that a breakdown of these informal experiences might justify regarding some clients as 'other treated' subjects.

Conversely, and bearing in mind the work of Rees [46], close investigation of experimental-group subjects might reveal poor levels of service from professionals. This observation is really a call for the analysis of factors within groups. Some of these factors are qualitative, but it is a delusion to think that qualitative factors can be excluded from social research. The larger danger comes from assigning numerical indices to human judgements and then forgetting just what the numbers stand for. One or two of the early effectiveness studies, involving special project workers, do not even address the question of what other, perhaps perfectly-adequate sources of run-of-the-mill professional help the control group might have availed themselves of.

Another set of problems concern the assignment of outcome indicators. I have already tried to quash the myth that the earlier generation of studies relied exclusively on narrow quantitative measures, but this remains a contentious issue for social workers. Quite simply we have never been used to specifying in advance the sort of criteria by which we could assess success or failure. Consequently it is regarded as brash even to speak of successes, and students and staff members are often talked out of 'over-pessimistic' interpretations of outcome by their supervisors. Because we never fail we never succeed, and this renders the profession vulnerable to political and administrative decisions based on ideology rather than evidence. This issue goes beyond the topic of experimental research. It is ironic that the two groups who have tried to remedy this problem, experimenters and behavioural social workers, are often reviled for their 'mechanistic' views [47]. Flexible, all-embracing outcome indicators (notions much favoured by the profession: such as people 'coming to terms' with things) are a contradiction in terms; almost anything can occur and they remain unthreatened. There are a few studies which rely too much on quantitative indicators, most have a sensible mixture of 'hard' quantitative and 'softer' qualitative measures.

Of course, indicators are not the same as outcomes; they 'stand for' outcomes. Usually they are a necessary but by no means sufficient condition of useful change. A large increase in school attendance without any accompanying reports of better classroom performance or satisfaction with the curriculum on offer, would be a poor indicator of success in a School Social Work project. But equally inadequate would be high scores on an 'educational satisfaction scale' without any sign that pupils were willing to attend the place! Similarly, while a Community School with a low rate of recidivism might just possibly be a Fagin's kitchen where the inmates learn to evade detection, a school with a high rate of recidivism has a tough case to answer. The indicators used in experimental research need interpreting and examining on their merits, study by study, but it is the profession which needs to change its attitudes (and its behaviour) about tests of outcome [48].

Bearing these difficulties in mind, the possibilities for a further extension of experimental research in Britain might be listed as follows:

(1) The government and the profession could foster a bolder attitude to controlled experimentation. The worst risks to clients could be mitigated by the provision of a minimum 'fire watching' service to the control group and a consequently more detailed statistical analysis of results. Indeed there would be no shortage of candidates for these minimum-intervention control groups since this is all that many client groups receive already. The difficulty might be in finding resources for the enhanced level of service required if the experimental group is to have a chance of producing better results.

(2) Not all social work carries high risks. After-care services to the mentally ill and mentally handicapped; services to schools and to young delinquents through intermediate treatment groups and special projects could all be evaluated through non-intervention comparisons. After all, in the case of the last two or three examples, a positive policy of non-intervention has strong advocates [49] and, hard though it may be to acknowledge, we may not be withholding anything of great value.

(3) Novel patterns of service could be singled out for special attention by local authorities. This happens already to some extent: e.g., attempts to evaluate professonal foster parent schemes or to compare the effects of conciliation work with standard count procedures [50]. The point here is that experimentation needs to be built into such new schemes.

(4) We have an urgent need for evaluations of the broad-based, practically-minded, patch-based social work which has emerged in Britain over the last decade: the mixture of advocacy, resource creation, welfare-brokerage, casework, social control, and support for self-help initiatives suggested by Davies [51] and the Barclay Report [16].

(5) Greater use could be made of 'defector control' designs (see Fig. 2) but here there would need to be an accompanying concern to investigate client differences. This design has the advantage that only clients whose problems 'fit' the agencies' services are studied and the social workers are not therefore being asked to take on all comers. The disadvantages are the problem of the non-comparability of clients, and that assessment alone may have a therapeutic effect on some clients.

(6) Therapy-wait or staggered service designs can be used to evaluate short-term intervention. Experimental and control subjects are divided into cohorts and compared at the end of a given period, say two months; then the controls receive services themselves as necessary. Attention has to be given to the distorting effects of 'drop outs', and 'spontaneous remissions' of problems – particularly in designs where the last control cohort forms the experimental group for the next comparison.

(7) Social workers could use single case experimental designs to evaluate their cases. These devices need no control group and practitioners and clients are directly involved in assessing the results of any work done.*

(8) An alternative policy to all the above would be to recognise that freedom to innovate and take risks in the interests of service-development might, sadly, have to remain largely the province of the voluntary sector, or take place through the 'purchase of service contracts' envisaged by the Barclay Report. However this is hardly what Seebohm [52] had in mind when he referred to the personal social services as '... large scale experiments in helping those in need', going on to observe that '... it is both wasteful and irresponsible to set experiments in motion and to omit to record and analyse what happens'.

RECENT DEVELOPMENTS IN EXPERIMENTAL RESEARCH

The results of experimental research conducted between 1973 and the present day add up to something of a change in our fortunes. Some of this work has been reviewed by Reid and Hanrahan [53] and to their selection one would wish to add the studies by Folkard et al [42], Shaw [43] Gibbons et al [44], Fowles [53], Sinclair [54] and Rose and Marshal [55]. Note the difference in tone from the gloomy conclusions of the Mullen and Dumpson/Fischer period [53]:

'All but two or three of the 18 studies yielded findings that could on balance

---

* These evaluation methods are the subject of an accompanying article in this volume.

> be regarded as positive. How does this success rate compare with that of the earlier studies? When the same criteria for assessing outcome are applied to the pre-1973 experiments we find that less than a third produced findings that could be regarded on the whole as positive. The difference is heartening.'

Many things have changed apart from reported outcome in the latest cohort of studies, particularly the methods and the patterns of service delivery of the social workers whose actions were being observed. Reid and Hanrahan attempt to identify the main differences in their review, and my conclusions about the original work match theirs in most respects. The most notable differences in the services supplied are as follows:

(i) The influence of behavioural methods is most evident, and given the large independent literature on the successful application of these principles [36] [56], it is pleasing to see social work beginning to align itself with the general trends of the research literature [57].

(ii) The main influence of behaviourism is mixed with other trends established in social work literature over the last fifteen years; the modern tendency to choose a series of smaller scale, more realistic goals and to pursue them in sequence rather than working for long periods on more diffuse objectives. The concern in these studies seems to be to 'shunt' the clients out of the vicious circles in which they are caught up, or to provide an early experience of successful problem-solving that will itself have motivating effects. In this, the work reviewed is consistent with a number of important trends in cognitive and behavioural psychology [35] [58].

(iii) The principles of time-limited service, with close monitoring of results as they accrue, are well established in this work [5] [44].

(iv) On this issues of monitoring progress (an approach to which according to consumer research and one or two specialist studies [6] [40] [59] [60] [61] clients, if not their social workers, are well-disposed), it is obvious that workers in many of the contemporary studies are choosing methods and styles of work that maximise the feedback they can get from clients. Objectives appear to be negotiated more openly than previously, and although there is evidence of disagreement between clients and workers on certain priorities, these are more likely to be concluded in rational terms. The wants/needs dilemmas and consequent patterns of miscommunication of a generation ago [41] are markedly less of a feature in these later studies. Here are Reid and Hanrahan's impressions of the implications of this 'contractual' and task-oriented approach [53]:

> 'The practitioner secures from clients commitments to undertake specific problem-solving actions. What is to be done and what is to be gained from doing it are clearly explicated and the client is engaged as a voluntary collaborator. Within this approach are apparently potent ingredients for bringing about change.'

(v) Though much of the work studied has a contractual flavour, there are also examples of behavioural contracting per se in this sample. The experiment by Stein and Gambrill [62] (N=200) featuring behavioural contracting as a means of securing the rehabilitation of children in foster care is one example. This is an exemplary study both in its methodological rigour, its size and scope, and in its relevance to modern child care practice. A study seeking to test the same principles [63] but using the predelinquent children who have spawned so much American research, achieved similarly positive results. The economy of the work in these later studies is staggering by comparison with the huge investments of counselling time of earlier work [8] [24].

(vi) Reid and Hanrahan point out that a number of these later studies (about 40%) feature group work. Certainly, clients are seen in groups, and this is an interesting change of emphasis. In the social skill training studies in particular, this is only half the story. It is also important to note the powerful effects of rehearsal and direct positive feedback on performance, which (if happening to take place in a group setting) are likely to be amplified by it when things go well [64] [65].

Turning to the methodologies of these second-generation experiments there are a number of interesting differences. These may be summarised as follows:

(i) In general the samples are much smaller, reflecting the rather more detailed approach to outcome measurement. More work is done on fewer clients.

(ii) In just under half, one is rather more certain of what exactly is on trial and how it is expected to have its effects. There is a skew towards the behavioural and quasi-behavioural approaches – the specific methods of which, as Reid and Hanrahan [53] note, are somewhat easier to describe. This ease of description is not just an artefact of these approaches; the advantage is the result of considerable effort on the part of theorists and therapists alike. The situation in this most important of considerations in social work effectiveness research is clearer, but the old problem still haunts us: last time we were not quite sure what didn't work; this time we are *somewhat* surer of what does.

(iii) Some of the positive conclusions being drawn about the social skills studies are, in my view, exaggerated and premature. They contain only in-group and/or role-performance measures of change. Psychological studies have already shown us very clearly that behaviour is remarkably situation-specific. From a social work point of view, whether these useful increases in the skill-repertoire of individuals amount to anything in the world outside the group, is of the utmost importance. The 'softness' of some of these evaluation methods detracts from the optimistic conclusions that have been drawn for the total sample.

(iv) More positively, the new research does reveal that a long looked-for development in experimental methodology is actually taking place; the researchers are concerned to monitor the appropriateness of outcome indicators so that there is a much better fit between the input and output sides of the experiments. Also in these experiments, the researchers are more often actively involved in the services they are seeking to evaluate and develop rather than having the status of outside 'referees'. Whether this development carries dangers of 'experimenter effects' and subjective judgement consumers of the research must judge for themselves from the published reports.

CONCLUSIONS

1. Social work researchers (and this is very little realised) were in at the very beginning of the experimental evaluation of therapeutic approaches. Delays in implementation have occurred because of the difficulty of digesting a large amount of unpalatable material, and because of the sheer range of the profession's theoretical affiliations. Whenever the logical relationship between particular research and particular patterns of practice has proved too taxing, there has been endless scope for moving on to new (and as yet, untested) affiliations.

2. Social work research jumped the gun back in the fifties and sixties. The riskiest of all possible methods of evaluation were applied – in my view because certain attitudes of theoretical chauvinism led people to believe that the results would be clearly and overwhemingly positive. Moreover, experimentation has the trappings of Science, where careful description, detailed work on single cases and with small groups and developmental research do not. Therefore we were (and to some extent are still) attempting to measure the dimensions of something that is not well understood.

3. The state of affairs referred to above is particularly unfortunate, in that rather than seeing the largely negative results of this premature application of experimental methodology as due to the inadequacy of the social work methods being studies,

failure has been attributed to the research methods themselves. Many people, asked to choose between science and the old time religion have chosen the latter.

4. Our need now is for detailed description of social work services and the reactions of clients and others to these; for developmental, illuminative, and action research that seeks to draw lessons for practice as it proceeds. Then, when we feel that a particular set of well-understood, well-described and differentiated, apparently consumer-satisfying, theoretically consistent practices are available (certain well-developed intermediate treatment programmes spring to mind) an experimental check becomes appropriate.

5. Finally, the question arises: research for whom? Probably our greatest failings lie in the area of research implementation, where, (despite excellent bodies such as the Social Services Research Group) we appear to lack the institutions and arrangements to ensure: (a) the systematic dissemination of findings, and (b) that research designs get built-into our services. Nevertheless, there are definite signs of progress in this regard, certain local authorities and certain universities (Sheffield, London) are beginning to demonstrate that they take this issue of the routine evaluation of services more seriously [66].

References

1. Mullen, E.J. & Dumpson, J.R. Evaluation of Social Intervention. Jossey Bass, London, 1972.
2. Fischer, J. 'Is Casework Effective? A Review' Social Work. Vol. 18, 5-20, 1973.
3. Fischer, J. The Effectiveness of Social Casework. Charles C. Thomas, Springfield, Illinois, 1976.
4. Levitt, E., Beiser, H.R. & Robertson, R.E. 'A follow Up Evaluation of Cases Treated at a Community Child Guidance Clinic' American Journal of Orthopsychiatry. Vol. 29, 1959, 337-347.
5. Reid, W. & Shyne, A Brief and Extended Casework. Columbia University Press, New York, 1968.
6. Goldberg, E.M. Helping the Aged. George Allen & Unwin, London, 1970.
7. Cabot, R.C. 'Treatment in Social Casework and the need for Criteria and for tests of its success and failure' Proceedings of the National Conference of Social Work. 1931.
8. Powers, E. & Witmer, H. An Experiment in the Prevention of Delinquency; The Cambridge Somerville Youth Study. Columbia University Press, New York, 1951.
9. Thomas, E.J. 'Selecting Knowledge from Behavioural Science' in Bartlett, H. et al Building Social Work Knowledge. New York, National Association of Social Workers, 1964.
10. Johnstone, E.C. et al 'The Northwick Park Electro-Convulsive Therapy Trial' Lancet, Dec. 20/27, 1980.
11. Kuhn, J.S. The Structure of Scientific Revolutions. University of Chicago Press, Chicago, 1962.
12. Sheldon, B. 'Theory and Practice in Social Work: A Re-examination of a Tenuous Relationship' British Journal of Social Work. Vol. 8, No. 1, 1978.
13. Bowl, R. & Fuller, R. A Study of Research in Social Services Departments. University of Birmingham, A Report to the DHSS, 1982.

14. Pincus, A. & Minahan, A. Social Work Practice: Model and Method. Peacock, Itasca, Illinois, 1973.

15. Specht, H. & Vickery, A. Integrating Social Work Methods. George Allen & Unwin, London, 1978.

16. Barclay Report Social Workers: Their Role and Tasks. Bedford Square Press N.C.V.O., London, 1982.

17. B.A.S.W., The Essential Barclay. British Association of Social Workers/Social Work Today, Birmingham, 1983.

18. Raynor, P. 'Rhetoric and Reality in Social Work' Community Care. 22, 3, 1979.

19. McCabe, A. The Pursuit of Promise. Community Service Society, New York, 1967.

20. Berleman, N.C. & Steinburn, T.W., 'The Execution and Evaluation of a Delinquency Prevention Programme' Social Problems. Vol. 14, 1967, 413-423.

21. Blenkner, M., Bloom, M. & Neilson, M. 'A Research and Demonstration Project of Protective Services' Social Casework. Vol. 52, 1971, 489-506.

22. Cohen, P. & Krause, M. Casework with the Wives of Alcoholics. Family Service Association of America, New York, 1971.

23. Most, E. 'Measuring Change in Marital Satisfaction' Social Work. Vol. 9 No. 1, 1964.

24. Miller, W.B. 'The Impact of a Total Community Delinquency Control Project' Social Problems. Autumn 1962, 188-191.

25. Geismar, L. & Krisberg, J. The Forgotten Neighbourhood. Scarecrow Press, Metuchen, New Jersey, 1967.

26. Behling, J. An Experimental Study to Measure the Effectiveness of Casework Service. Ohio State University, Columbus, Ohio, 1961.

27. Hudson, W.W. 'Special Problems in the Assessment of Growth and Deterioration' in Fischer, J. (Ed.) [3] op.cit. Ch. 10 (see also Ch. 4).

28. Polemis, B. 'Is the Case Closed?' in Fischer, J. (Ed.) [3] op.cit. Ch. 12.

29. Lakatos, I. & Musgrave, A. (Eds.) Criticism and the Growth of Knowledge. Cambridge University Press, Cambridge, 1970.

30. Clare, A. Psychiatry in Dissent. Tavistock, London, 1980.

31. Ullman, L.P. & Krasner, L. Psychological Approach to Abnormal Behaviour. Prentice Hall International, Englewood Cliffs, New Jersey, 1969.

32. Kendall, R.E. 'Psychiatric Diagnoses: A study of how they are made' British Journal of Psychiatry. 122, 1973, 437-45.

33. Brewer, C. & Lait, J. Can Social Work Survive? Temple Smith, London, 1980.

34. Truax, C. & Carkhuff, R. Towards Effective Counselling and Psychotherapy. Aldine Press, Chicago, 1967.

35. Bandura, A. Social Learning Theory. Prentice Hall, Englewood Cliffs, New Jersey, 1977.

36. Rachman, S.J. & Wilson, G.T. The Effects of Psychological Therapy. Pergamon Press, Oxford, 1980.

37. Bergin, A.E. 'The Deterioration Effect' Journal of Abnormal Psychology. 75, 1970, 300-302.

38. Palmer, E. 'Matching Worker and Client in Correction' Social Work. Vol. 18 No. 2 London, 1973.

39. Sainsbury, E. & Nixon, S. Social Work in Focus. Routledge & Kegan Paul, London, 1982.

40. Rees, S. & Wallace, A Verdicts on Social Work. Arnold, London, 1982.

41. Mayer, J.E. & Timms, N. The Client Speaks. Routledge & Kegan Paul, London, 1970.

42. Folkard, M.S. 'IMPACT' Home Office Research studies. Nos. 24 & 26 HMSO, London, 1975 and 1976.

43. Shaw, M. 'Social Work in Prison' Home Office Research Study. No. 22 HMSO, London, 1974.

44. Gibbons, J.S., Butler, J., Urwin, P. & Gibbons, J.L. 'Evaluation of a Social Work Service for Self-Poisoning Patients' British Journal of Psychiatry. 133, 1978, 111-118.

45. Eysenck, H.J. 'The Effects of Psychotherapy: An Evaluation' Journal of Consulting Psychology. 16, 1952, 319-324.

46. Rees, S. Social Work Face to Face. Arnold, London, 1978.

47. O'Hagan, K. 'Not Truth but Persuasion' Community Care. 28.7 1983.

48. Popper, K. Conjectures and Refutations. Routledge & Kegan Paul, London, 1963.

49. Schur, E.M. Radical Non-intervention: Rethinking the Delinquency Problem. Prentice Hall, Englewood Cliffs, New Jersey, 1973.

50. Coventry Social Services 'Evaluation of a conciliation service for separating couples and the families' Unpublished policy document, 1983.

51. Davies, M. The Essential Social Worker. Heinemann, London, 1981.

52. Seebohm Report. Report of the Committee on Local Authority and Allied Personal Social Services. CMND. 3703, HMSO London, 1968.

53. Reid, W.J. & Hanrahan, P. 'The Effectiveness of Social Work' in Goldberg, E.M. & Connelly, N. (Eds.) Evaluative Research and Social Care. Heinemann Educational, London, 1981.

54. Sinclair I, Shaw, M.J. & Troop, J. 'The relationship between introversion and response to casework in prison setting' British Journal of Clinical Psychology. 13, 1974. 51-60.

55. Rose, G. & Marshall, T.M. Counselling and School Social Work: An Experimental Study. John Wiley, New York, 1975.

56. Sheldon, B. Behaviour Modification: Theory Practice and Philosophy. Tavistock, London, 1982.

57. Fischer, J. 'The Social Work Revolution' Social Work. May, 1981, 199-207.

58. Seligman, M.C.P. Learned Helplessness: on Depression, Development and Death. Freeman, San Francisco, 1975.

59. Willer, B. & Miller, G.H. 'Client Involvement in Goal Setting and its Relationship to Outcome' American Journal of Clinical Psychology. Vol 32, No. 3, 1976.

60. Sainsbury, E. 'The Monitoring of Field Social Work Practice with People Suffering from Mental Ill Health and their Families' in Goldberg, E.M. and Connelly, N. (Eds.) Evaluative Research and Social Care. Heinemann Educational, London, 1981.

61. Sheldon, B. 'Goal Analysis: Do You Know Where You're Going?' Community Care 6:8 1977.

62. Stein, J. & Gambrill, E. 'Facilitating Decision Making in Foster Care?' Social Service Review. 51, 1977, 502-11.

63. Stuart, R.B., Jayratne, S. & Tripoki, T. 'Changing Adolescent Deviant Behaviour through Reprogramming the Behaviour of Parents and Teachers: An Experimental Evaluation' Canadian Journal of Behavioural Science. 8, 1976, 132-44.

64. Schinke, S.P. & Rose, S.O. 'Interpersonal Skill Training in Groups' Journal of Counselling Psychology. 23, 1976, 442-8.

65. Berger, R.M. & Rose, S.D. 'Interpersonal Skill Training with Institutionalised Elderly Patients' Journal of Gerontology. 32, 1977, 346-53.

66. Sheldon, B. (1987) Implementing the findings of Social Work Effectiveness Research. British Journal of Social Work, in press.

Cost Effectiveness Evaluation in Social Care

David Challis, Martin Knapp and Bleddyn Davies

INTRODUCTION

In recent years two research traditions in social care have gradually moved closer together. Evaluative research has conventionally focused almost exclusively on the *outcomes of alternative packages or programmes of care* (although rarely adequately measured), to the neglect of the resources that make such care a possibility. At the same time financial appraisal has concerned itself, with equal myopia, with the resources and costs of services without consideration for the effects of such services on clients and their significant others. Only relatively recently have these two concerns – the effectiveness of care and the associated costs – been considered simultaneously. Accompanying this gradual conflation have been a trend towards greater specificity in the conceptualisation and measurement of *effectiveness (or outputs)* and a willingness to broaden the definition of cost to include the indirect and individual resource burdens associated with care. In this paper we want to consider the present position of evaluative research from the rigorous perspective of cost benefit or cost effectiveness analysis (CEA). In doing so we will draw selectively on the more detailed discussions and illustrations of this perspective that we have presented in Challis and Davies [1] and Knapp [2].

CEA is just one of several evaluative techniques that are employed in social care research. Where it differs from other techniques is in its logical extension of the principles underlying those techniques to the examination of the full range of causes and effects [3]. The common theme of all evaluative research is to *inquire if a particular project or course of action is worthwhile and economic evaluation is no different in this purpose*. The difference is the meaning attached to the term 'worthwhile'. Economic evaluation, and particularly CEA, also shares a common basic assumption that political and administrative forces alone cannot be relied upon to generate efficiency or 'value for money'. It does not seek to replace the sound or educated judgement of the decision maker, based as it is and as it must inevitably be on political priorities. Weisbrod [4] has made the point that this technique will never 'make decisions', but if it is vigorously pursued it will 'make decisions better informed'.

In principle, CEA is simplicity itself. The costs of a project are compared with the benefits, outputs or effects. If two or more care programmes of projects are vying for selection, the project with the greatest effect for given cost is to be preferred. Effects and costs which fall to or upon any member of society are to be included and are to be measured in some common units to allow efficiency comparisons to be made. It is not restricted to answering questions about the criterion of efficiency. Increasingly, evaluations using this technique have sought to examine and comment upon the distributional implications of the proposed policies whose efficiency characteristics are apparently the primary focus of interest. However, CEA cannot provide answers to all the questions posed by decision makers, nor has it ever been claimed that it can do so.

Williams [5] suggests that CEA might usefully be employed to answer questions of the following kind:

(a) What care service is more or most appropriate in given circumstances?

(b) When should care be provided?

(c) Where should care be provided?

(d) To whom should care be provided?

(e) How should care be provided?

THE PRODUCTION OF WELFARE

The production of welfare model, which is closely related to the theory of production familiar to the economist, provides a powerful framework within which to comprehend the complex relationships between resource inputs, non-resource inputs, costs and outputs [1] [2] [6]. The production of welfare perspective distinguishes five components. Final outputs measure the changes in individual well-being, adjustment, quality of life, and so on, compared with the levels of well-being (etc.) in the absence of a caring intervention. In other words, *final outputs measure* the degree of *success* of a care unit or carer in meeting its objectives. In contrast, intermediate outputs are operationally defined in terms of the care services themselves, rather than the effects of these services on clients. For example, the level of provision of home help services or of residential care for mentally handicapped children is an intermediate output.

On the other side of the production relationship are the inputs. Resource inputs are the conventional factors of production. In the case of social care services the principal resource inputs include staff, physical capital (including buildings and vehicles), provisions and other consumable items. Associated with them are the costs of social care provision. In contrast, the non-resource inputs are those determinants of final and intermediate output which are neither physical nor tangible: they are embodied in the *personalities, activities, attitudes and experiences* of the principal actors in the social care process, particularly the care staff and the clients themselves. Obvious examples of non-resource inputs, therefore, are the characteristics of the social environment (the 'caring milieu') and the dependency, personality and health characteristics of clients.

The distinction between resource and non-resource inputs is an important one, both for causal argument and for policy formulation. The resource inputs are most often stressed in policy and planning documents, but it is a common assumption among professional and practitioner groups, and among some associated policy-makers, that non-resource factors are the more important. Certainly most of the social work and social care literature has focused upon the latter. However, to neglect the influence of the resource inputs is to limit the practical usefulness of any research concerning the association between non-resource factors and outputs. Differences in resource inputs will be partly responsible for observed differences in the extent to which care objectives are achieved, both because of their direct influence upon a client's welfare and because of their indirect influence through the configurations of social environments that they make possible. Equally, many of the influences of the resource inputs upon final outputs are mediated through and by the non-resource inputs. For example, the potentially detrimental effects of a poorly designed or inadequately staffed residential home may be ameliorated by a particularly supportive or stimulating caring environment. It is the resource inputs which enter the financial accounts of social care agencies and which, in the economist's terminology, have identifiable 'opportunity costs'. Cost, in fact, is the fifth component of the production model and can be seen as a shorthand term for the resource inputs entering the production relation.

Maintaining the distinction between these concepts allows us to state the basic premise of the production of welfare approach:

> Final and intermediate outputs are determined by the level and modes of combination of the resource and non-resource inputs.

This approach provides a sound basis from which to undertake a social care evaluation, and particularly a cost effectiveness analysis. All too often evaluative research has no clear conceptual grounding, which must inevitably constrain its eventual impact on policy and practice.

THE STAGES OF COST EFFECTIVENESS ANALYSIS

It is useful to distinguish six stages for a CEA:

(a) separate or define the alternatives to be analysed,
(b) list the likely costs and effects (or outputs),
(c) measure the costs and effects,
(d) compare the costs and effects,
(e) qualify or revise that decision in the light of risk, uncertainty, and sensitivity, and
(f) examine the distributional implications of the alternatives.

It should be noted that there is no unique CEA methodology; the analysis must always be adapted to fit the particular policy or practice question that is being studied.

Specify the Alternative (The Evaluation Question)

The exact nature of the range of policy choices facing care providers needs to be made explicit at the very beginning, and the question that the CEA will address should be made clear. It is crucial to get this question right, for once selected the nature of the whole study is determined. Are we concerned with whether or not to provide service A, or are we choosing between service A and service B, or are we considering how best to combine A and B? In some instances constraints on either policy or practice narrow the range of options right down, perhaps to a single procedure. We might then use the CEA framework to consider how much of this procedure is optimal. The evaluation of alternatives must be valid and sensible. It has often been remarked that false comparisons are made between residential and other forms of care because for some clients there is really (currently) no option to residential provision. We should avoid inappropriate 'blockbuster' questions, comparing service mode X to service mode Y, but be prepared to examine much more sensitive and finely specified research questions: for which cases and in what circumstances is one service 'better' (more cost effective) than another?

Comparison of service alternatives should be based upon realistic prospects. For example a scheme to enable elderly people to remain at home should be compared with the realistic alternative that would otherwise be received. Only a proportion of the population at risk of institutionalisation actually enter institutional care. Therefore to compare the costs (actual or predicted) of care at home with residential care costs is likely to exaggerate any apparent advantage of the community alternative. Nonetheless some studies have done this [7] [8].

List the Likely Costs and Effects

At the second stage, all the likely costs and effects need to be listed or enumerated, although no attempt is made to measure them just yet. Even if a cost or effect is considered to be immeasurable it should still be listed so as not to be forgotten in the final consideration of the results. This listing is not straightforward. Costs and effects are not as distinct as often suggested, either in theory or in the practical analysis. Take, for example the discussion of 'residential versus community care' for the elderly. One important cost of community care is the burden and strain borne by relatives and neighbours. But the removal of this burden is also a benefit of residential care, and so the researcher must be careful not to double-count it. There is thus a preliminary classification problem to overcome.

A helpful approach to the comprehensive listing of costs and effects is to distinguish 'interest groups'. Challis and Davies [1] specified nine 'interest groups' which might incur costs or enjoy benefits as a result of a scheme to provide care in the community for frail elderly people. These reflected a plurality of interests:

the elderly person,
informal carers,
the Social Services Department,
other local authority departments (e.g. housing),
the National Health Service,
the Department of Health and Social Security,
private and voluntary welfare agencies,
the guardians of public expenditure,
society as a whole.

Costs fall on the agency directly responsible for care (the local authority social services department, private or voluntary organisation), on other agencies such as the local authority housing department, the National Health Service or the probation service, and on the client, relatives and neighbours. These costs are incurred either directly or indirectly. Among the direct costs are those immediately and readily attributable to clients or groups of clients through local authority accounts. Thus it is possible to obtain without undue difficulty the average weekly cost of residential care for elderly people. It is much less easy to obtain estimates of the indirect costs such as those associated with social work teams, and with peripatetic or occasional NHS resources, and those incurred by clients and their relatives.

Almost all evaluations and commentaries concern themselves only with direct costs incurred by the providing agency. Some evaluators and some social care managers might argue that they are not concerned with costs incurred by other organisations or by clients. This is really rather short-sighted because many of these other costs fall directly to the local authority (for example, via the housing department) or to the taxpayer (for example, via the NHS). Actually, there are probably few managers or practitioners who would argue against the principle of including these other costs, but budgetary constraints and procedures often mean that they have to take decisions which minimise their own costs even though there may be a more than equivalent increase in costs incurred by other agencies or clients. There is thus a need to consider a wide range of cost accounts. Wright, Cairns and Snell [9] for example, recognised 'the importance of the informal caring network but ... did not attempt to cost its contribution ... because our research sponsors [the DHSS] requested us not to do so'. The informal care costs are responsble for a substantial amount of variation in aggregate community care costs. Similarly, Glass and Goldberg [10] produce a clear specification of the issues faced in a cost effectiveness evaluation of psychiatric services but mention only two costs accounts, 'the patient and the family' and 'the rest of society'.

If we now turn to the effectiveness or the outputs of care we can distinguish those enjoyed by clients, those enjoyed by people directly associated with clients such as relatives and neighbours, and those enjoyed by other members of society with a general concern for the well-being of clients and their carers. The listing of effects should range widely over all objectives and should take account of the different, and possibly conflicting, views of the different actors in the care system. Certainly client views must not be neglected. However, some studies have not considered output measurement at all, making the heroic and tendentious assumption that effectiveness does not vary between care modes. For example, some previous evaluations of British social care that have boasted the title 'cost benefit analysis' were really nothing of the kind. Wager [7] and PA International Management Consultants [11] simply conducted cost-cost studies and their total neglect of outputs does a disservice to the cost benefit or cost effectiveness tradition. Inadequacies of this kind can easily mislead and create a bad impression. Some studies can only cover a limited range of costs and effects because of constraints imposed by limited research resources, and the availability of staff. This can be seen in the study of home nursing

[12] where a statement of patient satisfaction appeared to be the only effectiveness measure. This may in fact have led to the understatement of the relative efficiency of home nursing.

The recent proliferation of 'Value For Money' studies conducted by firms of management consultants and accountants provides ample evidence of the ease with which grossly inadequate research specifications and reports gain lucrative commissions. Worse, they demonstrate a poverty of understanding among decision makers (see, for example, Audit Inspectorate [13] [14]).

Measure the Costs and Effects

At the third stage there are two steps: the quantification or measurement of the costs and outputs that have been listed, and their subsequent valuation in monetary terms. The technique of cost effectiveness analysis does not attempt to place monetary values on the outputs. Costs are to be measured in terms of opportunities foregone. If each of the resource inputs and outputs 'has an identifiable price over the lifetime of the project, if the project does not affect the price of any relevant good, if the prices of all relevant goods are set in a competitive market, and if none of the relevant goods (inputs or outputs) is a collective good', then valuation is a simple task [15]. One does not need much prior familiarity with the social care services to realise that none of these conditions is likely to hold in practice, and the researcher needs to seek ways around violations of them. In the terminology of welfare economics we seek shadow prices (see Knapp [2] Chapter 7.).

Recent studies have shown greater precision in their specification of costs and outputs, and greater clarity in their assumptions and estimations. This is well illustrated, for example, in the study of hospital, residential and domiciliary services for the elderly undertaken by Wright and his colleagues [9]. Particularly efforts have been made in the last few years to specify the costs and effects experienced by 'informal carers' [16] [17]. But there are still very few empirical estimates on which to base policy or practice (among the few are Baldwin [18] and Challis and Davies [1]). A recurrent theme in empirical research is that most researchers are surprised by the difficulty encountered in obtaining reasonable cost and effectiveness indicators, again reflecting (in part) an inadequate conceptual basis.

Compare the Costs and Effects

Having faithfully followed the recommendations of the first three stages we would have obtained a series of cost and effectiveness measures for each project or service package under review. Typically a new project requiring substantial capital investment will have high cost in the first one or two years followed by a period of low costs, whilst there may be no outputs at all until the service is in operation. Similar time profiles for the costs and outputs might be observed for preventive services. We therefore need to be able to compare costs incurred today with outputs enjoyed tomorrow, and the comparison is not immediately straightforward. We generally prefer one pound today rather than tomorrow because we have a whole day between now and then in which to use the money, a set of options not available tomorrow. This is the concept of time preference and allows us to 'discount' or weight future costs and outputs so as to render them comparable with present costs and outputs.

The discounting of future values back to the present time is simply the reverse of compounding interest and we use the term discount rate rather than interest rate. The researcher must select a suitable value (or set of values) for the discount rate, which is intended to measure society's rate of time preference and to reflect the alternative uses of the resources allocated to the proposed project or service. In fact, the Treasury recommends a particular numerical value for use in public sector CEAs. However, the choice of discount rate is crucial and most cost effectiveness analysts will examine the implications of more than one numerical value [2] [19] [20].

Up until now our description of the stages of a CEA applies with equal validity to a cost benefit analysis. The difference between the two is that no attempt is made in a CEA to place monetary values on the outputs. It is assumed that costs may be distinguished from outputs or benefits, and that the latter are not reducible to monetary measures 'as a matter of practice, or should not, as a matter of principle' [20]. Thus the CEA technique aims to show how a given level of benefit can be achieved at minimum cost (or maximum benefit at a given cost). Difficulties may arise with more than one output or benefit, especially when these benefits are not systematically or consistently related to each other. 'Rates of exchange' between benefits have been suggested. In this way it would be possible to calculate the 'cost per unit of output' for each project (having suitably discounted both elements back to the current period) and use this as the decision rule. Most economists would agree with Sugden and Williams [20] that CEA is of most value when 'choosing between mutually exclusive ways of achieving a particular, very clearly defined benefit'. It cannot, however, be used to say whether or not the benefits of a project or procedure actually outweigh the costs. What it can do is ensure that a full range of costs is estimated and that measures (but not values) are sought for all relevant dimensions of output. The information thus gathered can then be presented in such a way as to make plain the efficiency and distributional implications of the alternatives under consideration and allow policy makers to make the necessary trade-offs. For example, the analyst could supply comprehensive cost estimates for two alternatives, call them X and Y, with the cost of X exceeding the cost of Y. He could also supply detailed output measures (actual or predicted) for these alternatives. The decision maker must then decide whether the greater cost of X is outweighted by the greater benefit of Y. In so doing, of course, he is supplying the missing valuations.

An extremely useful technique at this stage is the method of multiple regression analysis. This technique allows the researcher to examine the simultaneous effects of outputs on costs for different levels of the non-resource inputs. This method was used by Challis and Davies [1], who examined the effects of health, dependency, levels of informal care and housing upon the cost of obtaining different levels of the two outputs, subjective well-being and quality of care for the elderly. It was therefore possible to calculate the cost of achieving combinations of two facets of wellbeing for frail elderly clients with quite different characteristics. In this way the research specification approaches quite closely the reality of care, where non-resource inputs (personal and environmental characteristics) influence staff decisions about the levels of resources needed to achieve outputs.

Sensitivity Considerations

The costs and outputs calculated for the various projects are usually expected or predicted values, and their prediction is always likely to be subject to some error however carefully undertaken. It is therefore important to qualify the decision rule and its recommendations by taking account of these errors. The researcher can allow for these by conducting a number of sensitivity analyses, computing the decision rules on different assumptions regarding the costs, outputs, rate of discount, and life span. These will indicate just how sensitive are the conclusions of the CEA to these different assumptions. Cost-effectiveness analysis is probably unique among evaluative techniques for its explicit and painstaking self-examination.

Distributional Implications

The final stage of the analysis is to examine the distributional implications of the alternative projects. CEA is a tool of efficiency analysis but need not, and indeed should not, ignore the equity issues raised by its policy indications or recommendations. Until quite recently most analysts were content to ignore equity considerations, but there is a swelling undercurrent of opinion and practice today which emphasises the role of the cost-effectiveness analyst in this regard. It would be wrong for analysts not to make clear the distributional implications of alternative projects, procedures or services for individuals in different socio-economic or income groups, for individuals in different areas of the country, for individuals with different needs and for the different 'interest groups' distinguished earlier. However, it would be equally wrong for the analyst to subsume equity under efficiency and use the CEA as a vehicle for his own prejudices. In some cases, of course, the distributional implications of a project may be too small to be of consequence, although this should be checked and not assumed.

IS COST EFFECTIVENESS ANALYSIS SUITABLE FOR SOCIAL CARE?

This description of cost effectiveness analysis has highlighted two things: the technique is less straightforward than some writers would have us believe, and it harbours a number of difficulties of both theory and application. Should we therefore abandon any attempt to apply it in the evaluation of social care? It is our belief that it should not be abandoned, but we do need to think carefully about its application and about the interpretation of its results.

There are inevitably some rather specific problems associated with the definition and measurement of costs and outputs, the choice of a suitable discount rate, the selection of the criteria for choosing between alternative projects, and so on. There are also some more general problems of research ideology. These include arguments about the inclusion or exclusion of the distributional consequences of alternative projects and the role of the analyst in the decision making process. We shall say nothing about the first set of difficulties. They are not unimportant, but they are all fairly self-contained and have all received some consideration in the literature. Furthermore, many – indeed most – are shared by all social care evaluations. Many of the criticisms raised against the cost-effectiveness technique are criticisms directed either at evaluation per se or at the evaluation of social care. Some of them are out of date, criticising or expressing reservations about aspects of the evaluation which have been successfully resolved by methods such as the production of welfare approach. Many of them are difficulties which are only avoided in alternative evaluative methodologies by making unacceptable assumptions about reality. If the principles of the production of welfare perspective are generally held to be reasonable, if the need for obtaining measures of the 'success' of care is accepted, and if the scarcity of resources is acknowledged so that benefits foregone (the opportunity costs) are considered as well as benefits received, then the usefulness of CEA cannot be denied. 'The question is not whether such analyses are desirable, for in one form or another – formal or informal – they cannot be avoided, but how to do the analyses in a useful manner' [21].

Some of the criticisms voiced about CEA have been born out of a misunderstanding of the true nature and intent of the technique and of the scope of its applicability. CEA will not help us choose between the expansion of care facilities for the elderly and the provision of more day nursery places for the under fives, nor does it claim to do so.

Two other common misconceptions about cost benefit and cost effectiveness analyses are that they only consider monetary items and/or that they attempt to place monetary values on items that are 'priceless' or 'beyond money'. The first thing to notice is that some items are only without prices by historical accident. Blood, for example, was not marketed in Britain until 1983 when the NHS introduced charges for private hospitals (and then the 'market' was very limited), and is marketed in many other countries. Just because an item is not marketed in our society does not mean that it can never be marketed although we might feel that it ought not to be marketed.

Secondly even if one does reduce all costs and benefits to monetary values – and it is our belief that this is not essential and, given our lack of knowledge about some services, not always feasible – this does not imply 'that an increase in the national income is the overriding goal of social policy' [22]. If some items (particularly outputs) cannot sensibly be valued in monetary terms then cost effectiveness analyses can still be employed, and to good effect. Of course, decision makers are attaching implicit valuations to these items. Whenever a social worker, home help organiser, residential homes' manager, social services director, or government minister allocates resources between services or clients a decision has been made as to relative costs and benefits of the competing claimants on those resources. Whether the values underlying these allocations are 'correct' is obviously a value judgement. The aim of the CEA, therefore, is to make these values explicit so that decisions might be more consistent and better informed.

Another criticism of CEA basically reduces to the contention that no information is better than some information. Buxbaum [23], for example, asks; 'Why should their (decision makers') collective minds be able to evaluate each piece of information, weigh it, balance it, and put together a better judgement? It is possible for information to overwhelm decision makers and distort decisions.' What Buxbaum [23] does not demonstrate is that decision makers make worse use of 'some information' than they do of 'no information'. Of course, if the information fed to them is itself misleading or misguided then the resultant policies might be totally wrong, but this is not the point that he is making. Our own interpretation of the available evidence is that policies based on 'no information' are demonstrably worse (in the sense of being irrational, inefficient, and contrary to the stated aims of policy makers) than those informed by evaluation studies.

Underlying Buxbaum's [23] argument is the view that:

> 'Political pressure to limit social welfare expenditure has converted economic analysis into the budget-cutter's rationalisation ... At present, it is probably wise to reject economic analysis and pursue political action to alter the political context. When the nation is restored to the pursuit of both efficiency and improved social welfare, rational decision making may be tried again.'

This association of cost effectiveness analysis (or perhaps even efficiency in general) with expenditure cuts is common. However, efficiency is a valid and justifiable objective whatever level of expenditure decision makers are planning. 'Cost benefit analysis has a dual function. It assists the decision maker to pursue objectives that are, by virtue of the community's assent to the decision making process, social objectives. And by making explicit what these objectives are, it makes the decision maker more accountable to the community'[20].

CONCLUSION

Cost effectiveness analysis is more an art than a science, more a way of organising thought than of mechanistically allocating resources. It should seek to uncover extant value judgements, and not unthinkingly impose those of the analyst or the politician. It cannot replace the judgements of decision makers but it can supplement and inform them. It can help the decision maker formulate his policy questions sensibly and logically and then provides a range of answers from which the decision maker might choose. If the decision maker misinterprets these answers it is the analyst's responsibility to point this out. It is not, however, his responsibility to determine policies. The interplay of economic appraisal and political priorities is the most sensible way to proceed. It is possible too, within the CEA framework, to tackle other strategies of evaluation such as pluralistic approaches. [25]

Some critics of the CEA approach point to an increasing tendency 'toward using (it) in areas where costs and benefits (effects) are more easily expressed in pecuniary terms' [23]. This might lead, it is argued, to the diversion of resources to areas where effectiveness or efficiency has been demonstrated and away from areas where it has not. Leaving aside the lack of evidence to support this view, and the naivety that is attributed to decision makers, the sentiment expressed is an important one. In fact, it has really only been the application of the CEA technique in areas where output or effectiveness measurement is most problematic which has won converts in the social care field:

> 'The hard-nosed approach of those who talk in terms of cost benefit and management by objectives has been disconcerting, as it has seemed to reflect a preoccupation with money rather than people, an attitude that people's needs must be tailored to financial considerations instead of financial resources being stretched to meet people's needs. However, as this approach developed into the idea of a goal-oriented social services system, I cannot argue the concept. In fact, I only wish that it had been generated and developed within the field, instead of from outside' [24].

References

1. Challis D.J. and Davies B.P. 'Case Management in Community Care', Gower, Aldershot. 1986; Davies B.P. and Challis D.J. 'Matching Resources to Needs'. Gower, Aldershot, 1986.
2. Knapp, M.R.J. Economics of Social Care. Macmillan, London, 1984.
3. Levine, A.S. 'Cost Benefit Analysis and Social Welfare Program Evaluation' Social Service Review. 42, 1968, 173-183.
4. Weisbrod, B.A. 'A Guide to Benefit Cost Analysis as seen Through a Controlled Experiment in Treating the Mentally Ill' Discussion Paper, Institute for Research on Poverty, University of Wisconsin, Madison, 1979.
5. Williams, A. 'The Cost Benefit Approach' British Medical Bulletin. 30, 1974, 252-6.
6. Davies, B.P. & Knapp, M.R.J. Old People's Homes and the Production of Welfare. Routledge and Kegan Paul, London, 1976.
7. Wager, R.A. Care of the Elderly. IMTA, London, 1972
8. Dunnachie, N. 'Intensive Domiciliary Care of the Elderly in Hove' Social Work Service. November 1979, 1-3.
9. Wright, K.G., Cairns, J.A. & Snell, M.C. Costing Care. Joint Unit for Social Services Research, Sheffield, 1981, 23-24.
10. Glass, N.J. & Goldberg, D. 'Cost-benefit Analysis and the Evaluation of Psychiatric Services' Psychological Medicine. 7, 1977, 701-707.
11. PA International Management Consultants. Cost Benefit Analysis in Social Services for the City of Leicester. Mimeograph, 1972.
12. Gibbins, F.J., Lee, M., Davison, P.R., O'Sullivan, P., Hutchinson, M., Murphy, D.R., & Ugwu, C.N. 'Augmented Home Nursing as an Alternative to Hospital Care for Chronic Elderly Invalids' Brit. Med. J. 284, 1982, 330-333.
13. Audit Inspectorate. Social Services: Provision of Care to the Elderly. HMSO for the Department of the Environment, London, 1983.

14. Audit Inspectorate. Social Services: Care of Mentally Handicapped People. HMSO for the Department of the Environment, London, 1983.

15. Hellinger, F.J. 'Cost Benefit Analysis of Health Care: Past Applications and Future Prospects' Inquiry. 17, 1980, 204-215.

16. Equal Opportunities Commission. Who Cares for the Carers? EOC, London, 1982; Platt S., Weymann A., Hirsch S. and Hewett S. 'The Social Behaviour Assessment Schedule: Rationale, Contents, Scoring and Reliability of a New Interview Schedule", Social Psychiatry, 15, 1980, 43-55.

17. Nissel, M. & Bonnerjea, L. Family Care of the Handicapped Elderly: Who Pays? Policy Studies Institute, London, 1982; Platt S. 'Measuring the burden of psychiatric illness on the family: an evaluation of some rating scales', Psychological Medicine, 15, 1985, 383-93.

18. Baldwin, S. 'The Financial Consequences of Disablement in Children' Working Paper 76.6/81, Social Policy Research Unit, University of York, 1981.

19. Pearce, D.W. & Nash, C.A. The Social Appraisal of Projects. Macmillan, London, 1981.

20. Sugden, R. & Williams, A. The Principle of Practical Cost Benefit Analysis. Oxford University Press, Oxford, 1978.

21. Weisbrod, B.A. & Helming, M. 'What Benefit Cost Analysis Can and Cannot Do: The Case of Treating the Mentally Ill' in E.W. Stromsdorfer and G. Farkas (Eds.), Evaluation Studies Review Annual. Sage, London, 1980.

22. Booth, T.A. 'Some American Lessons for Social Services Researchers' Social Services Research Group Journal. 11, 1981, 12-24.

23. Buxbaum, C.B. 'Cost-benefit Analysis: The Mystique Versus Reality' Social Services Review. 55, 1981, 467.

24. Shyne, A.W. 'Evaluation in Child Welfare' Child Welfare. 55, 1976, 5-18.

25. Smith G. and Castley C. 'Assessing Health Care: A study in Organisational Evaluation', Open University Press, Milton Keynes, 1985.

Pluralistic Evaluation

Gilbert Smith and Caroline Cantley

INTRODUCTION

One of the main problems in writing about evaluation is that as soon as the term is mentioned, the readers – be they planners, professionals, administrators or research workers – tend to jump to conclusions about what the term means, even though that conclusion may not accord with what the writer has in mind. In seeking to explain an approach to evaluation research which we term 'pluralistic evaluation' we have frequently encountered this difficulty. It seems to arise because thinking about the whole topic is so deeply permeated by certain crucial presumptions that an approach which departs from these presumptions is inclined to meet with the reaction that it cannot really be described as evaluation at all. In this chapter we shall argue that it can. Indeed we shall suggest that some, at least, of the starting points for much evaluation in the field of health and welfare policies are so mistaken and misleading, that only by radically revising them can we rid evaluation methodology of many of the confusions with which it is now bedevilled.

Our discussion will therefore run along the following lines. First we shall make explicit some basic premises which appear to permeate thinking about service evaluation. Second we shall refer to a good deal of recent work in the social sciences that leads us to question these starting points. Third we shall set out the difficulties that we believe evaluation research must now confront. Fourth, we shall outline the main features of pluralistic evaluation as a way of confronting these problems. We shall describe briefly a worked example of pluralistic evaluation. We shall list what seem to be some of the strengths of this approach. In conclusion we shall detail some outstanding problems. Our view is, however, that the direction of future debate must be a quite radical departure from the lines that have characterised much discussion in the past. Future developments will be inhibited if planners, administrators, professionals and researchers are reluctant to abandon existing stereotypes of what evaluation entails.

SOME PREVAILING PRESUMPTIONS ABOUT EVALUATION

There is a danger that in setting down some prevailing presumptions about evaluation and then criticising them, we may be accused of establishing a 'straw man' only for the purposes of our current argument. Our response is twofold. We believe that the design of much current evaluation, especially in the health and social services, does evidence heavy influence of the climate that we shall describe. Also, in negotiating support, access and cooperation for evaluative research and in feeding back the results of evaluation work we have been confronted [1] with presumptions about evaluation which reflect the following:-

1. Planning is a rational process. It is presumed that service development proceeds along the broad lines of problem identification - suggested solution - established criteria of success - implementation - measurement of outcomes - evaluation - feedback to modified solution. Of course it is widely acknowledged that such a rational mode of planning frequently breaks down in practice. Nevertheless evaluation is still discussed as though it did occupy such a place in the establishment of novel services.

2. Organisations have goals. Although it is readily agreed that goals may conflict and different groups may hold different objectives for a programme, evaluation is considered on the presumption that specific criteria for success will be available from the programme goals, and that the implications of the evaluation exercise will be self apparent when setting results against the original aims.

3. Policy statements are more or less reflected in 'the policy' as it is effected and evaluated. Again, it is widely acknowledged that there is a difference between official statements of policy intent and the effected policy in implementation, but in suggesting that something should be evaluated, it is generally presumed that the nature of that 'something' is relatively clear and need not enter the design of the evaluation exercise.

4. Policy takes significant account of the results of evaluative research. It is well appreciated that the ideal picture of evaluation feeding smoothly back into the policy process does not occur entirely smoothly. However if difficulties occur these are taken to be part of a separate stage of the enterprise, usually termed 'research implementation'. Evaluative projects are launched in a climate of optimism about their effects.

5. The experimental methods of the biological and physical sciences are a model to be followed in health and social service evaluation. Evaluation should emulate the

clinical trial. It is fully appreciated that this perspective may cause difficulties but these difficulties are seen, as it were, as technical problems that can be solved within the framework of what is seen as 'scientific' study.

6. Systems of health and welfare services are to be explained as essentially functional social systems [2]. Such a model features the high level of integration of the separate parts of the system and minimises the importance of a plurality of competing interests or the disruptive and central role of conflict between competing groups. This evaluation is seen as a part of the social processes of achieving harmony and unified system functioning and not as a part of competition, conflict, or the use of exchange and power in social care [3].

SOME PRESUMPTIONS ABOUT EVALUATION CALLED INTO QUESTION

These presumptions about evaluation have been prevalent for some time and have been fostered by the expansionist climate which has been a feature of the health and especially personal social services during the 1970's. That climate is now changing and with it must come some re-examination of the nature and role of evaluative research. Perhaps even more important is the fact that during the past few years some significant developments have taken place within the Social Sciences in which service evaluation has its theoretical and methodological roots. These developments have implications for the presumptions that we have just listed and leave evaluation research with significant problems.

1. The efficacy of many services is seriously in doubt. In spite of repeated efforts there are few convincing accounts of the achievements of social work intervention beyond the provision of strictly practical assistance [4]. There is grave doubt as to whether many psychiatric services provide anything other than drug assisted custodial care. Juvenile delinquency programmes probably do not reduce recidivism rates. Many post-war housing policies have been abandoned and their worst creations demolished even before the loans which financed them have been paid off. In spite of major changes in the educational system significant race, class and gender variations in achievement persist largely as a function of home environment [5]. Cumulatively, such findings endow evaluation research with new political significance placing it in a more controversial role than it may have occupied in the past.

2. Within the sociology of organisations the model of organisational functioning which rests upon the dominance of the idea of the organisational goal has been so heavily criticised that it is now generally obsolete. It is not simply that the goals of most organisations are multiple, confused, mutually exclusive or at least in conflict,

difficult to locate and define and changeable over time. There is more to it than that. There is Albrow's [6] argument that the very nature of an organisational goal is an ideologically based view which represents the interests of senior management. There is Bittner's [7] devastating comment that organisational members cast and recast the goals and aims to justify action pursued in their own interests. There is Zimmerman's [8] account of the weakness of trying to explain organisational behaviour as rule governed in pursuit of the goal. Yet if a service organisation cannot be said to have an identifiable goal, evaluation research has problems in locating some criterion for evaluation and in setting the results of evaluation against a statement of the organisation's desirable performance.

3. Within social policy studies, pluralistic and conflict models have been advanced as powerful replacements to functionalist understandings of the policy process [9]. Such models stress the significance of varied and variable interests within the development of social policy and the varied power bases employed to advance such interests. Moreover any understanding of the policy process [10] then calls for a rather detailed understanding of the interaction of these interests, as early proposals move to implemented outcomes through stages in which they are transformed, interpreted, adapted, opposed and altered in numerous and varied ways. One central feature of these models is to argue that social policy studies have hitherto paid insufficient attention to the plurality of interests involved in developing health and welfare programmes, especially the interests of clients, patients, relatives, junior staff and other less powerful groups. The point is directly applicable to much evaluative research.

4. It is now widely accepted that there are important differences between the physical and social sciences. Most important, the social sciences study objects who themselves possess 'verstehen' (understanding) and, as voluntaristic actors within the system, have powers of interpretation and choice. There are too many moral and practical problems of controlling the data that are not a part of the experimental laboratory. Serious attention to the meanings which research subjects assign to their social world adds complication to the design of evaluation research. Qualitative data measuring validity must often replace highly quantified data sometimes preferred because of its apparent reliability. In practice the controls of the clinical trial are seldom available. Even quasi-experiments are often such poor substitutes for the real thing that we would be better using an entirely different kind of design. Moreover crucial features of the object of study are often obscured by forcing the study into an experimental design. The researcher ends up by imposing meaning on the data, complaining that if only the social world were different then he (or she) would be able to experiment.

5. Within political science and public administration the presumed rationality of traditional planning models has been heavily criticised. Much of the debate has centred around 'disjointed incrementalism' as an alternative [11]. The point of relevance for evaluation research is that if planning is not the logical process that rational models imply, then evaluation research designs can no longer rely on the inherent good sense of planners to recognise truth when they see it (in evaluative research) and take appropriate action.

6. Political philosophers have pointed to the relevance of notions of justice and fairness to the concepts of evaluative judgement. The debate is an extended one but House gives the flavour of the discussion.

> 'One of these influencing factors (on what the evaluation does) is the conception of justice that the evaluation and the sponsor of the evaluation hold, usually quite tacitly. What the evaluation believes is right and the prevailing conception of justice significantly affect the evaluation' [12].

Such a view conflicts with a view of evaluation as an activity which is a 'neutral', 'objective' or 'scientific' aid to management in planning and decision taking.

7. Evaluators themselves have become dissatisfied at repeatedly finding that the programme that they had been led to believe they would be able to evaluate was not at all like the programme they encountered when they started to evaluate it. Alternatively they proceeded with the evaluation as if it were, only to sink into a mire of methodological confusion as a result. Rein goes so far as to suggest that frequently there is no programme [13].

8. Generally social scientists have become less sanguine about the significance of policy research upon subsequent policy [14]. Certainly only the most optimistic (or naive) evaluators hold to what Bulmer calls the mechanical model [15]. Most view research, at best, as just one of a list of variables that may influence the future climate of decision making. It is very hard to locate examples of Government decisions attributable to research and equally hard to pinpoint the impact of any particular programme evaluation.

SOME PROBLEMS UNCOVERED BY QUESTIONING PREVAILING PRESUMPTIONS

In calling into question some major presumptions upon which evaluation research has been based we do generate a number of difficulties. Actually we do not generate them. They have been there all the time. Our argument is that past failures to uncover, make explicit, clarify and solve these problems, in part at least, account for the fact that much evaluation research has not had the impact upon service provision that we might have expected it to have.

Pluralistic evaluation is an approach which has developed in response to some of the difficulties which are now being uncovered. Our next task, therefore, is to state these problems as clearly as we can before proposing some solutions. The foregoing discussion means that we must now confront four tasks.

1. The controls of the clinical trial are very seldom available. Yet frequently the evaluation question is posed in the form, 'What would have happened if the programme being evaluated had not occurred?' How can alternative policies be compared the one with the other without the experimental control of numerous variables?

2. Frequently the nature of the programme that is to be evaluated is unestablished at the start of the investigation and anyway, typically it changes quite rapidly over the time especially if, as is often the case in evaluation research, it is a novel programme. As soon as we take seriously the point that official accounts of policy intent are only a partial guide to programmes in practice we face a problem of evaluators being able to declare that a programme does or does not 'work' but without being able to say what that programme is. So, how can the design of evaluation research cope with the fact that the object of the investigation is, typically, unestablished and likely to change quite significantly as the study proceeds such that the events and institutions being examined at the conclusion of the research are quite different from those at the start?

3. Since, frequently, it is not easy to locate any clear statement of the objectives of a new programme and since there are variable views from different groups about what constitutes 'success' in the programme's achievements, the evaluator has difficulties in selecting any criterion of evaluation that will command widespread acceptance. Indeed it is not clear how the evaluator can select any criterion at all for measuring 'success', apart from simply imposing an account of what he (the evaluator) considers the initiative should achieve. But that tactic is of little use if at the end of the research the judgements are dismissed by those responsible for the programme as based upon a view of what it should have achieved that they do not share. How can evaluators establish measures and criteria of success in the absence of agreement about policy objectives amongst those planning, providing (and in receipt of) the services?

4. Design for evaluative research must take more seriously the question of the relationship between the research results and the social policy impact of these results. It must pay more attention to what has previously been described as the task of 'implementation'. Since much evaluation research has been grounded in an inaccurate model of the policy process it is hardly surprising that its impact upon that process has been limited. How can the research design ensure that the relationship between research and decision taking in policy is part and parcel of the investigation from the start?

PLURALISTIC EVALUATION AS AN APPROACH TO THE EVALUATION OF HEALTH AND WELFARE SERVICES IN RESPONSE TO THESE CONCEPTUAL, METHODOLOGICAL AND POLITICAL DIFFICULTIES

We are arguing then that we must devise an approach to evaluation which is somewhat different from that which characterises much work in the area, if we are to overcome the difficulties that we have mentioned. The approach which we have termed 'pluralistic evaluation' is one such approach [16]. We shall give a general impression of what this approach entails by outlining its basic tenets before describing briefly one worked example of a study in which we have carried out such a plan.

The following are the main features of a pluralistic evaluation.

1. The approach is heavily informed by models of institutional functioning and the policy process which draw upon theories of political pluralism. Thus we are sensitised to the importance of varied group interests and power bases and the ways in which the plurality of interests interact in a system of checks and balances upon which the workings of the service are eventually based. This does not exclude an analysis of conflict as between two major (class) groups. But typically in the field of health and welfare services the constituent parties are more numerous than that. The approach is also heavily influenced by the 'subjectivist' stance within sociology [8] [17]. Thus we are sensitised to the importance of understanding the interpretations which professionals, planners, administrators, clients and patients place upon the operation of the agencies of which they are part.

2. Thus the research must identify the major constituent groups to the policy initiative and, throughout the research, compare them with each other, both in the ideological perspectives that they hold, and in their operational strategies.

3. In particular, we must collect data on these groups' interpretations and

perceptions of 'success' in service provision and assign to that data a central place in the evaluative analysis.

4. The study must document not only the plurality of notions of success but also the different groups' strategies as they strive to implement their own perspectives in their own interests. We take the view that an attempt to disentangle the meanings and pursuit of 'success' is an intrinsic part of the evaluation exercise.

5. Evaluative research must then assess the extent to which success (or failure) is achieved on each of the several criteria employed within the agency and in terms of the several meanings assigned to these criteria. Success is a pluralistic notion. It is not a unitary measure.

6. In consequence, pluralistic evaluation must embody the principles of methodological triangulation. Denzin [18] forcefully agrues that any study dependent upon a single data source is 'method bound'. The point of particular relevance to evaluation research is that each data source is interest bound (as tied to the interests of one group rather more than to the interests of another) and also ideology bound (as reflecting one group's perspectives on desirable modes of operation rather more than the perspectives of other groups). The debate on the use of official records and statistics best illustrates this point [19]. The constant use of as great a variety of different kinds of data ensures as far as possible that the research reflects the full range of interests, ideologies, interpretations and achievements abroad within the agency.

7. Thus, throughout, pluralistic evaluation offers an ethnography of the way the services develop and an explanation of this development (in terms of the pluralistic interests of participating groups) as well as (somewhat complex) conclusions about the success of these services on a range of criteria interpreted in various ways. Our claim is that the attempt to link the problems of an organisation as perceived by its constituents, to the performance of the institution's programme of service, constitutes evaluative material.

In practice, it is not easy to conform to these tenets. We believe, however, that the attempt is rewarding and productive of data that is rich for both explanatory and evaluative purposes. For pluralistic evaluation goes some considerable way towards solving the difficulties that we have discussed in the early part of this chapter. In the next section we describe briefly a study in which we have adopted this approach.

PLURALISTIC EVALUATION: A BRIEF ACCOUNT OF A WORKED EXAMPLE

As one illustration of the character of pluralistic evaluation we described an evaluative study of a new psychiatric day hospital which, in its conduct, followed the major tenets that we have outlined [20]. The study was commissioned with a view to evaluating the success of the service.

Generally, in designing the research we accepted the view that a conclusion is much stronger when supported by data from different sources and therefore adopted an approach of triangulating research methods. Throughout we interviewed as many different groups as possible, inspected hospital records, made transcripts of discussions and meetings and took field notes on observations and conversations. Sometimes our sampling was not as systematic as we would have wished but as a general rule we maximised 'richness' even at the loss of some 'rigour'.

The issues of qualitative versus quantitative data collection methods feature in much research literature. We regarded this debate as an artificial one. When we were able to quantify precisely, we did so. But a qualitative account which identifies important factors for measurement is a necessary prerequisite to any attempt at the quantification of variables and in some areas of our research we concentrated on this.

More specifically we collected the following data.

1. We interviewed the nurses, psychiatrist, doctor, social worker and other staff and administrators responsible for establishing and running the hospital. These interviews were semi-structured, focusing particularly on respondents' attitudes to the 'success' of the hospital and were tape recorded and transcribed.

2. We attended over a two year period many of the hospital meetings, held weekly to discuss patients, and collected field notes on the meetings. We also tape recorded a number of meetings some of which were fully transcribed.

3. We collated and studied a range of hospital records on a sample of all referrals and admissions to the hospital over a six month period. The documents include psychiatric domiciliary visit reports, social work assessment reports, medical assessment and continuous nursing notes.

4. We assembled a brief statistical account of referrals, attendance patterns of the hospital population and discharges over a two year period.

5. During the course of field work we were able to make some observations of the day to day life of the hospital and on the manner in which patients are serviced when they attend the hospital.

6. We interviewed relatives of 25 patients. These interviews were again semi-structured and asked relatives about their perceptions of the patient's problem and their experience of receiving services, generally and in connection with the Day Hospital in particular.

7. We attended over two separate periods of a year each, meetings of a Relatives Support Group held in the hospital. Apart from making field notes on these occasions we recorded several meetings and some of these recordings were transcribed.

It has also been a principle of our methods of data collection and analysis that the distinction between raw data and final report is by no means a rigid one. Thus throughout we accumulated working notes which were based upon our data but which themselves became sources of information for subsequent analysis.

The hospital that we were studying was designed to have and indeed did possess some genuinely novel features in the provision of day care for the elderly mentally infirm. Although not all aspects of the service are as innovative as the claims sometimes made for them, the degree of experimentation that is apparent (for example in opening hours, a relatives support group, transport arrangements) added weight to our views that a first task lay in documenting the nature of the service, before evaluating it. Planning documents gave only one view of what was expected in the institution and many crucial features of the service developed over time and in the process of implementing planning guidelines.

The ethnography of the Day Hospital draws on many of the above data sources and covers such matters as:

the building,
transport arrangements,
the complement and organisation of staff,
the patterns of admission and discharge,
and the regular routines and daily life of the hospital.

However it is important to note that the hospital changed considerably during the period of fieldwork, some three years over all. In important respects the services we were evaluating at the start of the project were different from those we were studying towards the completion of the research. And certainly there is a complex process of implementing policy initiatives. Indeed most features of the hospital are in this sense dynamic. As we have already noted this has important implications for the methodology of evaluation. Our data collection had to attempt to encompass these changes and proceses in the service.

A preliminary study of the Day Hospital revealed that a wide range of different professional staff are involved in providing services in this hospital including a social worker who plays a more significant role than is usually the case in similar health service settings. The perceptions of these professionals – consultant psychiatrist, day hospital nurses, ward nursing staff, social worker, occupational therapist, chiropodist, physiotherapist, administrators, attached community psychiatric nurse, vary and have implications for the way the hospital operates. Additionally because patients only attend on a limited number of days each week, they remain in contact with a number of 'community based' professionals – home help staff, general practitioners, area team and residential social workers, community nurses and occupational therapists – who also have some impact on the day to day activities of the hospital. Finally the patients themselves and their relatives, who are often heavily involved in providing care, must be considered as significant constituent groups. Naturally these groups vary in significance and those mentioned may not exhaust all the possibilities.

In studying the perceptions of these groups, we found that there were at least six separate ways in which 'success' for this hospital is given meaning and thus the hospital's objectives and desirable modes of operation specified.

Firstly, in defining success as provision of an integrated service, staff attach great value to good communication both within the hospital and between it and other organisations.

Secondly, in advancing the notion of success as 'patient flow', staff suggest that the hospital should reduce demand for inpatient beds, shorten waiting lists for these beds, prevent and delay admission to in-patient beds, facilitate the discharge of patients from related hospital wards and improve the use of particular categories of beds by the correct categories of patients. Above all 'silting up' both in the day hospital itself and in other parts of the hospital system to which it relates should be avoided.

Thirdly, in referring to the success of the hospital in improving the clinical condition of patients, staff assign to the hospital what is perhaps the most obvious objective.

Fourthly, staff define success as beneficial impact on related services in the overall system of health and social care for the elderly mentally infirm. This view implies that even if the hospital has no significant effect on the elderly patients themselves it might nevertheless be justified in the help which it offers social workers, general practitioners, community nurses or whatever.

Fifthly, a view of success as service to relatives dictates that services should be positively extended to give assistance to relatives in caring for patients both by providing emotional support and by educating them in how to manage the patient at home.

Finally in advancing the notion of success as quality of service staff point to a number of features of the hospital environment and staff attitudes which are desirable in their own right quite apart from whether there is any demonstrable effect upon the clinical condition of patients or in any other way. For example, the hospital should provide a pleasant stimulating environment for patients and staff should convey caring attitudes to patients and relatives.

Of course these approaches to the meanings of success are not necessarily mutually exclusive but they do imply different emphases in evaluating the hospital and they do entail on occasions different courses of action when they are used to dictate operational policies. They are also given very different meanings by different constituent groups within the hospital.

We can take 'patient flow' as a criterion of success as one example of these processes at work in the institution [21]. There is wide agreement that the ready admission and discharge of patients (thus avoiding silt up of the system) is important. However, this consensus is only a broad one, for within it each group perceives and pursues its own interests. On the basis of detailed consideration of our data on the pursuit of this overall objective by different groups we see that much of the hospital's work with patients cannot be understood if we presume that there is unambiguous advantage in a shared policy of having patients entering and leaving the hospital as rapidly as possible. It very much depends upon just which categories of patients are moving where, how, and with what consequences for what groups of staff, relatives and other patients.

For consultants 'patient flow' means essentially that the Day Hospital should avoid 'silting up' and so provide them with a constantly available option when considering how to dispose of referrals from GPs. The consultant uses a number of strategies in pursuing this end, including an active discharge policy, use of alternative services wherever possible and flexible use of a small number of hospital beds in close association with the Day Hospital. Nursing staff also have strategies for dealing with the 'silt-up' of the hospital. They negotiate with relatives their understanding of the terms of admission and they generally favour a rather selective approach to admission. However the interests of other groups in 'patient flow' do not always accord with those of consultants and nurses.

GPs' requirements are for facilities which will help them to cope with any elderly patients who are making, in their opinion, excessive demands on their time and energy. This brings them into conflict with Day Hospital staff who feel that they must retain selectivity in order to avoid silting up. For ward staff the major interest in 'patient flow' lies in enhancing movement out of in-patient wards through the Day Hospital, but this approach generates problems for the Day Hospital by blocking that part of the system if patients do not in practice move on. For the Social Worker the general principle of the need to maintain patient flow is tempered with concern for the needs of the family unit. The social worker may resist discharge if adequate relative support is not available for the patient at home. In this respect the social worker's interests are quite distinctly different in key respects from all other staff groups.

Finally, relatives too have their own perspective. Although there are exceptions, for the most part relatives have little interest in or expectation of discharge from the Day Hospital. In general staff perceptions of the advantages of 'turnover' and the benefits of discharge to patients and relatives are at cross purposes with the perceptions of the relatives themselves.

In attempting to assess the effectiveness of the hospital in achieving 'Patient Flow' we drew upon statistical and other records information to document patterns of patient movements into and out of the hospital and related services. We conclude that in one major respect, the hospital is a success: it does avoid silting up. However there are major qualifications. This judgement rests upon a particular definition of 'success'. For there is no substantial evidence on the clinical improvement of the majority of patients. The largest group of discharges is to long term care. There are comparatively few links in terms of patient flow with non-hospital services (especially social work). There is little evidence that the hospital has significantly reduced demand for in-patient beds. Moreover, success from the point of view of consultants and nurses has been achieved by adopting strategies which may well mitigate against the achievements of success as understood by other groups of staff and relatives involved in this system of care.

The achievements of the hospital on criteria other than 'patient flow' are equally complicated, ambiguous and inconclusive. The point of relevance to the present discussion is our general conclusion;

> 'So if we take multiple meaning seriously in service organisations, if we seek to display them in empirical detail, and if we describe also the associated tactics of interpretation, then, it seems, we give lie to the fond hope that a simple evaluation is ever possible. What emerges is a pluralistic account which is bound to show that on some criteria, given some meaning, and pursued by some group with some influence to some effect, the hospital, or whatever, is in some sense successful. In other senses and from other perspectives it is not. In short, an answer to the evaluative question is complicated, lengthy and detailed and we must set it out as fully as we can. But rather than proving to be an embarrassment, a pluralistic framework now serves an invaluable purpose; it helps us to structure this account' [21].

THE ADVANTAGES OF PLURALISTIC EVALUATION

We began this chapter by explaining that we advanced pluralistic evaluation primarily in response to some problems that it seemed difficult to solve in any other way. In bringing the chapter to a close we can list what seem to be a number of specific advantages of this approach to the evaluation of social work services.

1. It provides a complicated but realistic answer to the question of whether a service is successful or not. Much research has indicated that most health and welfare institutions fail to live up to their utopian ideals. The reasons for this are now quite well understood [22]. The professional providers and planners of a service are likely to eulogise over a service's performance. Pluralistic evaluation is likely to indicate that in some ways a service is a success and in some ways it is not. As a general comment that is trite. But if we know which aspects of the service are which, that is immensely valuable.

2. This form of evaluation has the potential to explain why failures in service provision occur. Most often this explanation will take the form of an account of which groups have been able to marshall power and resources to pursue their interests, and at what cost to other groups and other forms of service provision. Thus the ways in which service fails (by some criteria) are displayed by this form of evaluation, and not merely the service outcome.

3. This explanation (as an intrinsic part of the evaluation) opens the way for

change. Planners, professionals and administrators can see (if they so choose) which groups must be assisted and supported if their objectives and interpretations are to gain effect. Evaluation is limited if it cannot indicate how limitations and weakness can be rectified.

4. Pluralistic evaluation details some of the costs of success. Few operational policies are entirely free of unanticipated consequences and it is important to be aware of these consequences even when faced with what is apparently a 'successful' policy in general terms.

5. Pluralistic evaluation facilitates the implementation of research results. One major barrier to effective implementation of the policy suggestions of social research has always been opposition from groups who claim that the research design did not take into account their particular interests. Since pluralistic evaluation cannot be dismissed as dominated by the perspective of a limited group or groups, there would seem to be a greater chance of effective policy implementation of the research results.

6. Evaluative studies are often commissioned because the agency sponsors seek some 'neutral' or 'objective' assessment of the work. But this is hard to achieve since much evaluation is, implicitly, tied ideologically to a particular perspective on the services. Pluralistic evaluation stands some chance of remaining 'independent' and 'neutral' by taking sympathetic account of as many perspectives as possible.

SOME OUTSTANDING PROBLEMS

In conclusion we turn briefly to some problems that are outstanding in the theory and methodology of pluralistic evaluation. Some reference, if only brief, to these problems is important because, as we have argued earlier in this chapter, failure to acknowledge some of the implicit difficulties of evaluation has in the past been a cause of considerable confusion.

1. It may be a mistake to link the methods of pluralistic evaluation to the pluralistic model of policy analysis. The issue is whether it is possible to use pluralistic methods only within conflict model of policy analysis, or within any other framework. Some social commentators would argue that a pluralistic model is by no means universally adequate. But if pluralistic evaluation is limited to those institutions and policies of which a pluralistic model is adequate, the approach may not be as widely relevant as we have initially implied [23].

2. Pluralistic evaluation entails the heavy use of qualitative data. There is a problem in the implementation of policy recommendations that rest upon the interpretation of qualitative results. And although we have explained why pluralistic evaluation has some distinct advantages with respect to implementation it is clear that both the general approach of the method and, especially, qualitative data are far from the 'Scientific' study that many administrators and professionals expect. They may be resistant to them as a result [24].

3. Just as there is a problem of implementing results, so there may be a problem in obtaining the support of administrators and professionals in commissioning pluralistic evaluation.

4. It may be a mistake to view evaluation as a separate kind of social research. We have stressed that adequate evaluation should entail explanation. It has often been argued, equally forcefully, that explanation in social science cannot avoid an evaluative component [25]. If these two arguments converge, the distinct features of specifically evaluative research may be mythical.

5. There is a particular problem of data exclusion in conducting pluralistic evaluation. We have argued that the perspectives of constituent groups are defined and their inclusion justified. The major danger is that in selecting these groups the investigator adopts a model of the institution and the policy process which is itself biased towards one particular set of interests.

6. Finally it may be that pluralistic evaluation is just a child of its time responsive to the political climate of the day. We have criticised much other evaluative work for merely reflecting the political climate of 'managerialism'. There may be ways in which pluralistic evaluation is a subject of a similar process, even if the results are different. The high degree of reflexive analysis is the main protection against that weakness.

NOTES

1. For example in studying some aspects of the Children's Panel system in Scotland and the reorganisation of British Social Work. See, for instance, Smith, G. & May, D. 'The appointment of the Aberdeen city children's panel' The British Journal of Social Work. Vol. 1, No. 1, 5-25: and Smith, G. Social Need: Policy, Practice and Research. London, Routledge and Kegan Paul, 1980.
2. The debate about functionalism within sociology has been an extended one. The social work literature has not been as aware of it as it should have been. Many of the current discussions about systems theory in social work seem to be unaware of arguments that have been well rehearsed elsewhere. For a recent text on functionalism in sociology, see the relevant section of Bilton, T. et al. Introductory Sociology. London, Macmillan, 1981.

3. Again, the social work literature would do well to draw on Blau, P.M. Exchange and Power in Social Life. New York, Wiley, 1964.

4. The difficulties are well illustrated by M. Goldberg's classic attempt, Helping the Aged: A Field Experiment in Social Work. London, Allen and Unwin, 1970.

5. Of course, these points are gross generalisations and their detailed substantiation is beyond the scope of this chapter. But the broad point stands. For some relevant discussion see:

   Clare, A. Psychiatry in Dissent: Controversial Issues in Thought and Practice. Second Edition, London, Tavistock, 1980; Baldwin, J. & Bottomley, A.K. Criminal Justice: Selected Readings. London, Martin Robertson, 1978. Especially Part V and Ch. 24, Bottomley, A.K. 'The Failure of Penal Treatment – Where Do We Go From Here?' pp. 238-244; Butterworth, E. & Weir, D. Social Problems of Modern Britain. London, Fontana, 1977. Section 5, 'Urban Problems'; Haralambos, M. Sociology: Themes and Perspectives. Slough, University Tutorial Press, 1980, Ch.5 'Education'.

6. Albrow, M. 'The Study of Organisations – Objectivity or Bias?' in Gould, J. Penguin Social Science Survey. Harmondsworth, Penguin, 1968.

7. Bittner, E. 'The Concept of Organisations' Ch. 17 in Salaman, J. & Thomson, K. (Eds.) People and Organisations. London, Longman for the Open University Press.

8. Zimmerman, D. 'The Practicalities of Rule Use' Ch. 9 in Douglas, J. (Ed.) Understanding Everyday Life: Towards the Reconstruction of Sociological Knowledge. London, Routledge & Kegan Paul, 1971.

9. See, for example, George, V. & Wilding, P. Ideology and Social Welfare. London, Routledge & Kegan Paul, 1976; Hall, P. et al. Change, Choice and Conflict in Social Policy. London, Heinemann, 1975.

10. Hill, M. Understanding Social Policy. Oxford, Basil Blackwell & Martin Robertson, 1980.

11. For a summary and comment on the debate see Smith, G. & May, D. 'The Artificial Debate Between Rationalist and Incrementalist Models of Decision Making' Policy and Politics. Vol. 8, No. 2, 147-161.

12. House, E.R. Evaluating with Validity. London, Sage, 1980.

13. Rein, M. From Policy to Practice Ch. 9, 'Comprehensive Program Evaluation' London, Macmillan, 1983.

14. Gandy, J., Robertson, A., & Sinclair, S. Improving Social Intervention. London, Croom Helm, New York, St Martin's Press, 1983.

15. Bulmer, M. The Uses of Social Research. London, Allen & Unwin, 1982.

16. So far as we are aware, this approach to evaluation is an original one. There is now a growing number of empirical studies in the field of health and welfare services, which incorporates a 'pluralistic' component within the research design, often in response to the difficulties which are encountered in, initially, pursuing a rather traditional approach. (For example, clear statements of aims are hard to find). However, not all researchers are prepared for the difficulties which a pluralistic stance, in turn entails. (As we have tried to show in this chapter the collection and interpretation of data can become extremely complicated) and we have observed a tendency to 'revert' to a traditional stance at key points in the analysis. The result is sometimes a muddle.

    One of the fuller reports of a study contributing to what the authors terms 'broadly-based or "pluralistic" approaches to the evaluation of health and social care interventions' is an account of an evaluation of a travelling day hospital for elderly mentally ill people conducted within the Social Services Research Intelligency Unit (SSRIU) at Portsmouth Polytechnic. For a fuller comment on this study see Smith G (Forthcoming) 'Review of N Evans (et al.) 'Something to look forward to' SSRIU Report No 15, Portsmouth Polytechnic, England', in *Ageing and Society*.

Much research pays serious attention to the perspectives of various groups within institutions. See, for a major example, Strauss, A (et al.) Psychiatric Ideologies and Institutions. New York, Free Press, 1964. But this is seldom cast in an evaluative framework.

We have located one important use of the term 'pluralism' in the context of evaluation. House [12] describes 'pluralistic/institutionists' who 'value participation of the people involved in the program'. An extended quotation is in order.

> '... this participation consists of collecting the viewpoints and opinions of various people about the program or policy at issue. The evaluator faithfully records and portrays their viewpoints. In this manner, the principles, criteria, and weightings of the people involved are used to judge the program. Of course, in selecting and emphasising some aspects and viewpoints at the expense of others, an inevitable occurrence, some of the evaluator's own principles come into play.
>
> In portraying the judgements of various groups associated with the program, this latter approach is pluralist not only in the philosophical sense of judging on the basis of several principles but also pluralist in the political sense of representing different political interests. Of course, the judgements of the participants and the evaluator are almost always intuitively balanced.
>
> The pluralist/institutionist theory of justice is the most commonsensical of all, but it leaves the evaluation subject to whatever principles and weightings the judges, whoever they are happen to employ.'(p.127)

But there are important differences between the approach House describes and pluralistic evaluation. In House's account the viewpoints of participants are the only source of data. Criteria and judgements are not clearly distinguished and the place of the evaluator's intuition is ambiguous. As House adds, critically;

> 'At one extreme, it threatens total command of the judging process by professional principles and at the other extreme, a complete relativism in which everyone's opinion is presumed to be as good as everyone else's.'(p.127).

These are exactly some of the difficulties that our suggestions seek to overcome. 'Pluralist/institutionism' bears only a tentative resemblance to pluralist evaluation.

17. Douglas, J.D. (Ed.) Deviance and Respectability: The Social Construction of Moral Meanings. New York, London, Basic Books, 1970.

18. Denzin, N.K. The Research Art in Sociology: A Theoretical Introduction to Sociological Methods. London, Butterworth, 1970. It is a pity that the title of this text implies that its relevance is confined to sociology, because it is not.

19. See, for example, Hindes, B. The Use of Official Statistics in Sociology. London, Macmillan, 1973; Bottomley, K. & Coleman, C. Understanding Crime Rates. Farnborough, Gower, 1981.

20. The research project from which this illustration is taken was funded by the Scottish Home and Health Department and was based initially in the Department of Social Administration and Social Work, University of Glasgow, and then in the Department of Social Administration, University of Hull. Valerie Ritman was also a member of the research team in Glasgow. For a fuller account of this project see Smith, G. 'Some Problems in the Evaluation of a New Psychogeriatric Day Hospital' in Taylor, R. and Gilmire, A. (Eds.) Current Trends in British Gerontology. Farnborough, Gower, 1982;

    Cantley, C & Smith, G. 'A Relatives Group in a New Psychogeriatric Day Hospital: A Research Note' The British Journal of Social Work Vol. 13, No. 6, 1983;
    Smith, G. & Cantley, C. With Ritman, V., 'Patient Turnover in a New Psychogeriatric Day Hospital: A Pluralistic Evaluation' Aging and Society. Vol. 3, No. 3, 1983.

    The final report on the study is published as Smith, G. & Cantley, C. Assessing Health Care: A study in Organisational Evaluation. Milton Keynes and Philadelphia, O.U.P. 1985.

21. This illustration and the list of six advantages that follows draws heavily on Smith, G. and Cantley, C. with Ritman, V. 1983 [20].

22. For an early statement see Etzioni, A. 'Two approaches to Organisational Analyses: A Critique and a Suggestion'. Administrative Science Quarterly. Vol. 5, 257–78.

23. We are grateful to an anonymous reviewer of Smith, G. and Cantley, C. with Ritman, V., 1983 [20] for making this point.

24. See Walker, R. (Ed.) Applied Qualitative Research, Aldershot, Hampshire, Gower for a fuller discussion of this point.

25. For the classic statement of the point see, Becker, H. Sociological Work: Method and Substance. Ch. 8, 'Whose Side Are We On?' Chicago, Aldine Publishing Co., 1970.

Issues in the Further Development of Evaluation in Social Work Services

John E. Tibbett*

The need for social work services to account for their activities and to examine closely and in a rigorous manner the scale and deployment of resources and methods used is extremely pressing. The pressure arises from several sources: the consequences of policies of constraint in public expenditure at a time of significant demographic change; the questioning of whether present forms of social work intervention produce desired outcomes; the demonstration that, in some areas at least, there are alternative modes of provision with real gains in cost effectiveness; a concern with standards of professional practice; and the increasing sophistication in the expectations of service users. If social work services are to project themselves successfully as a sector to which significant public resources are to be allocated and to which additional resources should be devoted if a consistently high standard of services is to be provided, then the efficacy of services has to be developed. Agencies require methods for the systematic assessment, control and redeployment of the often scarce and expensive resources at their disposal. Policies of incremental development on all fronts and 'managers muddling through' [1] are no longer appropriate in the current context in which personal social services operate.

In Britain we do not yet seem to have experienced the burgeoning of an 'evaluation industry' as has happened in the U.S., although terms like 'assessment', 'audit', 'appraisal' and 'evaluation' are rapidly becoming buzz words in social services agencies. All refer to processes for the systematic examination of events occurring in and as a consequence of the activities of agencies and their staff, with a view to formulating some kind of judgement about the relative value of the activity based more on firm data and less on whim or received wisdom. Such judgements should then allow improved decision-making about the development of the particular activities and any similar programmes. If evaluative work is not yet widespread in

* The views expressed in this paper are those of the author, and do not necessarily represent those of the Scottish Office.

British social work agencies there are nevertheless some excellent examples of such work [2]. There is also a lively debate about the range of methods and foci for this work, much of which is reflected in the earlier papers in this volume.

In this final chapter I want to discuss a number of general issues which are important if evaluative work is to become a more central part of social work than it is at present.

QUESTIONS FOR EVALUATIVE STUDIES

What kinds of knowledge should evaluative studies be seeking to elicit? Scrutiny of services for effectiveness and efficiency requires that a number of basic questions are addressed. These will include the following:

1. *Targeting*
   Are the social needs of the clients which services are to meet defined? Have the intended clients been clearly identified?

2. *Inputs*
   Are resources available at a sufficient level and in a suitable form to meet the needs identified?

3. *Process*
   In the delivery of services, are the standards required by statute, professional practice and efficient administration met?

4. *Output*
   Are the services as delivered consistent with original goals, procedures and standards?

5. *Outcome*
   Irrespective of the above, do the services meet identified client needs? Are there unanticipated consequences?

6. *Efficiency and Review*
   Not withstanding the 'successful' formulation and implementation of specific services, is the overall deployment of resources between client groups and between services consistent with the objectives of the agency?

Several observations relevant to the purpose of this paper may be made from this list of basic questions. In the first place, the variety in focus of evaluative work is potentially enormous. It can be concerned with either structural, procedural or outcome-orientated aspects of agency performance. It can be concerned with organisational or administrative factors or with professional content of agency functions. It may be concerned with strategic policy-making, the operational management of specific services, or with service delivery to individual clients. In the face of this variety there is a need for greater clarity than is often apparent in the formulation of those aspects to which any particular evaluative study is to be devoted. Loose formulations of a desire to know whether programme X 'works' do not allow systematic evaluation and tend to foster studies which provide inconclusive or otherwise unhelpful results.

Two further points arise from an appreciation of the potential range for evaluative studies. Different problems require different methods for their successful research. Thus there is a need for a wide range of techniques for evaluative work which will extend from large scale experimental or sophisticated pluralistic evaluations to carefully constructed single case studies. Studies may be based on economic data or 'hard' survey data, or on much 'softer' material drawn from observational work or reflection on practice. The papers in this volume illustrate the fact that 'evaluation' is not some monolithic research method, but a whole variety of processes which need to be carefully selected for the purposes of the investigation in hand.

It follows too, that evaluation is not the province of trained researchers. Whilst some applications will undoubtedly require these skills there are other situations where reliance on an 'outside' researcher may be less than ideal. For example, there is much to be gained both for the development of social work practice generally and for the development of individual social workers from the careful and systematic study of practice situations. In order to advance its standing as a profession with specific skills to offer, social work needs to embrace evaluative work as an integral part of practice to a much greater extent than is the case at present.

Even if due consideration is given to the precise formulation of the focus of interest of a piece of evaluative work, and this has led to the adoption of a suitable method of study to be undertaken by those best placed to do so, there are other issues which are likely to be faced where social work research in general needs to progress, and to which many evaluative studies will contribute. It is to these that I will turn in the remainder of this paper.

ASSESSING QUALITY OF CARE

The issue of the quality of care delivered in a service programme can arise in many contexts. For example, in residential care, does raising the staffing ratio increase the quality of care? In economic evaluations of provision, how does one know if two similar services are providing a comparable quality of care? How does an agency satisfy itself that its services are being consistently delivered to an oppropriate standard and according to the policies of the agency? All of these questions involve the concept of quality, but this may vary in its implications for evaluation. Indicators of quality in the first two examples are likely to be found in the analysis of the outputs and outcomes of service provision, whereas the third example is more concerned with inputs, that is with the specification of acceptable processes of good practice and the study of whether or not they are being achieved.

Clearly this latter aspect is of a very different order from the first. It is concerned with the equivalent for social work of quality control in industry. Whilst this may be an uncomfortable notion for some social workers, it is an essential element both in the maintenance of the credibility of professional standards and in agency control of its resources. There has been some real progress in developing methods for quality assurance, largely in America, and often in the context of hospital social work [3]. In essence these methods involve the development of a 'card' which stipulates the steps required for good practice in particular settings or in relation to particular problems, and then the examination of performance in a sample of cases in the light of the contents of the card. This examination is frequently conducted on the basis of a 'peer review', that is a group of workers studying the practice of their own team. It is claimed such methods are of benefit to the individual workers in their own professional development, and also provide a means of demonstrating the social work contribution to clients to other agencies. There is no reason in principle why these methods cannot be extended to most areas of social work practice.

ASSESSING OUTCOMES

The ultimate justification for social work services lies in its ability to meet client need. This is easily said, but because of the complexity of social need and of the concern to improve a client's general social functioning, the assessment of outcomes of social work intervention is notoriously difficult. Perhaps for this reason it is not often attempted, but it is a question which cannot be escaped in decisions about the deployment of resources or about the choice of methods to be employed.

The concept of 'outcomes' has to be unpacked. It can be pursued at a number of levels. Sainsbury [4], for example, has indicated the range of criteria for evaluation in his study of a community psychiatric service. They may be epidemiological measures, rates of referral to services, rates of admission to or contact with services, measures of cost-efficiency, ratings of the outcome of the illness, scores of the burden on caring families, or measures of the client's lifestyle. This range embraces both what have been referred to as intermediate outcomes, which are often measures of service output as identified earlier in this paper, measures of outcome in the short-term which relate to the resolution of particular presenting problems, and final outputs which relate to the way of life which follows from a service intervention for the client and his family. As one progresses through this list towards final outcomes so the problems of conceptual clarity and identification of appropriate and measurable indicators increase. Whilst there has been good progress in some areas in developing measures of outcome [5], there remains a need for much more work in this area.

ECONOMIC ANALYSIS

The drive for efficiency in the provision of social work services underline the importance of another relatively undeveloped approach to the evaluation of services. Gross [6] has recently provided a convenient summary of a variety of approaches to such analysis. He highlights the numerous theoretical and technical problems which beset cost-benefit and cost-effectiveness studies. The relatively easy part should be the measuring of direct service costs, but even here there are many problems arising from the way local authority budgets and cost control procedures are operated. It is the benefits or effectiveness side of the equation which generates the most severe difficulties, which relate partly to the problems of specifying professional inputs and assessing the extent to which goals have been achieved (output). Furthermore a comprehensive analysis needs to consider not only direct costs but indirect costs, and non-monetary social costs for those involved in the care process. The measurement of these presents formidable problems.

There are many alternative modes of analysis even if cost measures are available which themselves address slightly different questions and hence may have differing utility. Gross's paper demonstrates how the adoption of one cost reporting method rather than another may lead to quite different conclusions from the analysis.

DISSEMINATION AND UTILITY OF EVALUATIVE RESEARCH

The problems for evaluative research I have raised above are conceptual and technical ones which require urgent attention. But none of this effort will bear fruit in improved service delivery if its results are not disseminated and utilised. Some see evaluation facing a particularly hostile environment [7], from both policy-makers (who 'don't know and can't wait') and from service providers. Whilst evaluative work has come a long way in recent years its scope and bite has been limited. It is still the case that much of this work is essentially descriptive, and only rarely comparative. The potential in evaluative work will only be realised if a number of developments occur. These include:

- The funding of stable teams of researchers to work with social work agencies and professionals to address the theoretical and technical problems of evaluation outlined above;

- the earlier recognition of opportunities for evaluative work on the part of service providers allowing researchers to be introduced earlier into the planning of innovations;

- the recognition by employers that evaluation is an essential part of practice, and that an allocation of time to this work carries with it benefits for the agency;

- a greater emphasis in social work training on the importance for the development of practice of evaluative and quality assurance studies;

- further improvements in facilities for gaining access to evaluative work which is carried out in order that its implications can be more widely shared.

The potential payoff for the development of professional practice and for innovation in the organisation and delivery of social work services from attention to these points and hence for the systematic analysis of service provision is enormous. It is to be hoped that this collection of papers stimulates some progress in these directions.

References

1. Rees, S. & Wallace, A. Verdicts on Social Work. Edward Arnold, London, 1982.
2. Goldberg, E.M. & Connelly, N. The Effectiveness of Social Care for the Elderly. Heinemann, London, 1982.
3. Coulton, C.J. 'Quality Assurance for Social Service Programmes: Lessons from Health Care' Social Work. September 1982.

4. Sainsbury, P. 'The Problems of Evaluating a Community Psychiatric Service' Community Development Journal. Vol. 11, No. 3, 1976.

5. Challis, D. 'The Measurement of Outcome in the Social Care of the Elderly' Journal of Social Policy. Vol. 10. No. 2, 1981.

6. Gross, A.M. 'Appropriate Cost Reporting: An Indispensible Link to Accountability' Administration in Social Work. Vol. 4, No. 3, 1980.

7. Illsley, R. 'The Contribution of Research to the Development of Practice and Policy' in Elderly People in the Community: Their Service Needs. HMSO, London 1983.

Research Highlights in Social Work

No 3 Developing Services for the Elderly
2nd Edition
Edited by Joyce Lishman and Gordon Horobin
1 85091 002 2 Hardback
1 85091 003 0 Paperback

No 4 Social Work Departments as Organisations
Edited by Joyce Lishman
1 85302 008 7 Paperback

No 5 Social Work with Adult Offenders
Edited by Joyce Lishman
0 9505999 4 8 Paperback

No 6 Working with Children
Edited by Joyce Lishman
1 85302 007 9 Paperback

No 7 Collaboration and Conflict: Working with Others
Edited by Joyce Lishman
0 9505999 6 4 Paperback

No 8 Evaluation 2nd edition
Edited by Joyce Lishman
1 85302 006 0 Hardback

No 9 Social Work in Rural and Urban Areas
Edited by Joyce Lishman
0 9505999 8 0 Paperback

No 10 Approaches to Addiction
Edited by Joyce Lishman and Gordon Horobin
1 85091 000 6 Hardback
1 85091 001 4 Paperback

No 11 Responding to Mental Illness
Edited by Gordon Horobin
1 85091 005 7 Paperback

No 12 The Family: Context or Client?
Edited by Gordon Horobin
1 85091 026 X Paperback

No 13 New Information Technology in Management and Practice
Edited by Gordon Horobin and Stuart Montgomery
1 85091 022 7 Hardback

No 14 Why Day Care?
Edited by Gordon Horobin
1 85302 000 1 Hardback

No 15 Sex, Gender and Care Work
Edited by Gordon Horobin
1 85302 001 X Hardback

No 16 Living With Mental Handicap: Transitions in the Lives of People with Mental Handicap
Edited by Gordon Horobin and David May
1 85302 004 4 Hardback

No 17 Child Care: Monitoring Practice
Edited by Isobel Freeman and Stuart Montgomery
1 85302 005 2 Hardback